Where the Hell Were Your Parents?

A true story about what happens
when you let your kids run feral

by

NATHAN WEATHINGTON

D1468872

PROMONTORY
PRESS

Where the Hell Were Your Parents?

Copyright © 2014 by Nathan Weathington

Promontory Press
www.promontorypress.com

First Edition: May 2014

ISBN: 978-1-927559-40-6

Cover Design by Evan Pine
Typeset at SpicaBookDesign in *Old Style*

Printed in Canada

To my mom and dad.
Thanks for giving us a childhood
exciting enough to write a book about.

★

And to my boys.
I hope I can give you a childhood as
fun as mine, minus the felonies.

Table of Contents

I Hate Snakes

1982

8 years old

Sue Harris is a kind woman — I am glad we didn't kill her. She was morbidly afraid of snakes, a weakness she let slip at a dinner party with our family. My identical twin brother Brian and I recognized and communicated an opportunity between us in a millisecond using that magical twin telepathy crap everyone always talks about. When we were finally able to break away from the table, both of us had already worked out the entire play, making further planning unnecessary.

We were new in town. Our dad was the head football coach, which in Bremen, Georgia, is more important than the mayor, Wal-Mart, and the lady who turned tricks at the local truck stop all combined. Let's just say I found the movie *Friday Night Lights* a bit watered down. We were also twins, a bit of an oddity in a town of 3,500 people with only one other set at the time.

So, although we had not earned our notoriety, we were known. People knew we were Coach's sons the day we arrived in Mountain Shadows, a glamorous suburb outside of the booming Bremen metropolis. But in a few years the roles would reverse. My parents would soon be known as the parents of the Weathington Boys, a title they carried with an even ratio of pride, love, and shame.

Brian and I had a great childhood. Our parents loved us, supported us, and somehow found the strength to not beat the living ass out of us. I can only hope I'll have the same restraint with my two sons if they try to pull half the shit we did. Our parents gave us freedom kids today don't have; we could go anywhere and do anything, and we usually did it packing heat.

Our parents had the courage to allow us this independence, without cell phones or a GPS device planted in our rectums. They did not entertain us twenty-four hours a day, buy us video games, or have a day-timer for our extracurricular activities. Yes, this sometimes led to temporary boredom. Boredom, and the subsequent hell Bremen suffered as we entertained ourselves, was a recurring theme of my childhood, and thus this book.

Had our parents obsessively entertained us, a lot of people would have never met the Weathington Boys, which might have seemed like a blessing at the time. However, those same people would now be stuck talking about their lawns and the weather instead of telling an entertaining story about being fleeced as part of the Raccoon Removal Scam of 1987. Amusing ourselves with such projects provided valuable life skills. Although video games do build impressive thumb strength, keeping our virginity into our thirties seemed like a harsh tradeoff.

The combination of smothering parents, the Internet, and reality television guarantees this next crop of kids will be the dullest our planet has ever seen. If you are ever stuck in a serious situation at work or in life, maybe turn to the kid who knows which end of the gun is the business end, not the one with the highest score on *Dig Dug*.

Our parents were comfortable with us being rough around the edges and took pride in the fact that we had more bruises, tetanus shots, and fish hook accidents than the normal kids. They did not give in to the parenting peer pressure of the day. Other parents found them irresponsible as we ran wild and routinely damaged or lost their precious children. This peer pressure is escalating with my generation as we partake in a heated arms race to prove who can be the most responsible, and therefore, the safest parent.

This movement has led parents to push for playgrounds that are as exciting as hermetically sealed carrots in your Halloween bag. Where the hell is the zip line these days? Maybe it's harsh, but if your kid walks off the end of a plank ten feet in the air, chances are we needed to weed him out anyway or we might all end up as monster truck fans.

This safety movement has also led to an attempt to decrease stress in our kids' lives. We've removed grades from schools, scores from athletic events, and kids whose parents can afford the visit to the doctor can get their sweethearts untimed testing. And if little Johnny is still stressed by the untimed testing, we have some meds for that. Fast forward to these kids telling their first boss that it doesn't matter how long it takes them to stuff the Happy Meal.

The most extreme symptom of competitive parenting is baby sign language. This ridiculousness is somewhat self-explanatory. Lunatic parents have convinced themselves that their three-month-old is a master linguist despite the fact that they eat their own boogers. It might be hard to believe, but your kid smells like he said he shit his pants, not that he enjoys listening to Mozart's *Piano Concerto #17.*

My parents did their own thing when it came to parenting, mostly my mom's doing. My mom's childhood was less than spectacular to say the least. She was determined ours would be better, and man, it was. Now that I'm trying to figure out how the hell to raise two boys of my own, I frequently turn to her for advice. Her goal was for us to be independent and willing to take risks, and if that meant a few extra stitches and felonies, then so be it. She would not have allowed us to sit around Bremen, Georgia, after we graduated talking about our glory days over a case of PBR with the boys down at the local mud bog.

Sue Harris — our neighbor with the snake phobia — would not have accused my parents of over-parenting, not by a long shot. She volunteered to baby-sit us the day after that fateful dinner party. Things were going well — cupcakes, toys, and the high fructose corn syrup drink du jour. When the sugar-high dissipated, it was time to focus on the task at hand.

A week prior, while we were supposed to be having our souls saved for the umpteenth time at Bremen United Methodist Church, we snuck across the street to the Triangle store and purchased a plastic snake with the $3.25 we lifted from the offering plate. This was not your ordinary plastic snake. It was infinitely more believable than the holiness of our Youth Director, whom we all knew was sniffing enough glue to paper mache a revival tent. It was a dead ringer for a copperhead, and in case you're not up on your ophiology, a copperhead is a very poisonous snake that inhabits the southeastern U.S.

While playing in the yard, we carefully wove "Oscar" into Sue's grass.

"Do you think it will work?" I asked Brian.

"Well, only one way to find out."

Brian, being the gutsier of the two of us, kept it simple and believable.

"Snnnnaaaake!!!"

"Convincing," I said.

"Thanks."

It only took one call. Sue burst out the front door like a Greyhound trying to avoid the inevitable antifreeze hotdog. Her feet barely touched the ground. Imagine a hysterical woman on a pogo-stick running the forty yard dash with four-three speed. Impressive. If my dad had witnessed her performance, he would have asked her to try out for tailback. She reached the shed, snatched up some kind of quick-release weapon — which turned out to be a razor-sharp hoe — and returned in a single bound, weapon poised. Oscar was a goner.

During this unexpected athletic performance, I could barely control my excitement and I looked to Brian for support. He simply stood with his arms crossed, the picture of relaxation, with just the edges of his mouth slightly turned up. He already looked like a seasoned gangster. Picture Robert De Niro's character in *Goodfellas* as an eight-year-old, dress him in cutoffs instead of a suit, and you have Brian Weathington.

If Brian was a cross between *Goodfellas* and *Stand By Me*, I think that would make me Geordie, the lead character in *Stand By Me*. Geordie and I were both a bit more compassionate than our counterparts, tended to be the voice of reason, didn't like leeches on our balls, and when push came to shove would bring the crazy in spades.

Sue's attack on that plastic snake would have made any mongoose, or parent, proud. Before we could tell her it was a fake, Oscar was minced into hundreds of pieces. In a move describable now as Matrixesque, she leaped back to the front door and disappeared inside.

Complete silence. Cue chirping crickets.

"Wow," I finally gasped. "That worked way better than I expected."

"The best $3.25 we ever spent."

"We'll need to get another snake."

"Most definitely."

Sue never came back outside to check on us or even spoke to us from a window. We assumed she was in the fetal position somewhere in a closet. After picking up Oscar we strolled back home, our stroll quickly, yet unintentionally, becoming a strut. Once home, we cooked ourselves dinner and tried to see if we could descramble Skinomax.

As I was working the cable box over with a butter knife, our parents drove up. I flipped the channel to a nature documentary and jumped in my dad's recliner. As they walked in, my mom looked over, confused.

"What are you two doing here?"

"We came home for some dinner," I answered.

"Well, what did you make?"

"Pop-Tarts and Yoo-Hoo."

"That sounds like a well-balanced meal," my mom said in her most sarcastic voice.

"Are there any left?" my dad chimed in, detouring us off of my mom's original line of questioning.

6

"Stay focused, Larry. What did you do?"

"Well, do you remember Oscar our plastic snake?"

"You didn't."

"I'm afraid we did."

"You probably gave that poor woman a heart attack."

"Yeah, I think we scared her really bad. She chopped Oscar into a million pieces."

"Wow, I bet that was a sight," my dad said as his Pop-Tart dinged in the toaster.

"You're not helping this situation, Larry."

My mom appeared to be upset, although even at the time I did not feel it was sincere. She walked across the street to try to calm Sue down.

Tucked into our bunk beds, Brian and I laughed ourselves to sleep with stories about the short yet eventful life of Oscar the plastic snake. It was a noble death. We were born partners in crime, and the fact that we both found the same pranks entertaining only led to more trouble.

From that day forward, Bremen was our town; they were just livin' in it.

Where There's Smoke, There's Hoodlums
1983
9 years old

Mr. Sharp was a cantankerous old man — I am glad we didn't kill him. Or at least I don't think we killed him. Word had spread about the Weathington Boys, although apparently Mr. Sharp had not gotten the memo.

It was just like every other hot-as-hell summer day in Bremen. Dark, heat-soaking colors were avoided to prevent spontaneous combustion. We also never wore sun block; I guess it hadn't been invented yet, or least my parents had not heard of it. In summer, you would have had a hard time picking us out of most Mexican towns. Anyway, we lived too far away for cross-border antics like fireworks-smuggling or gun-running, which was probably for the best.

Compare this to today where my two sons are wearing white-boy sombreros with mud flaps in the back while having their entire bodies dipped in glue. We treat the poor boys like vampires, which, contrary to *People Magazine,* is not all it is cracked up to be.

Several normal, polite, church-going kids had joined Brian and me in hopes of either elevating their "cool" status or increasing their odds of playground survival. And that day we were heading to Big Creek, not to be confused with Little Creek on the other side of the neighborhood. Big Creek routinely had larger crawfish and a rope swing that would make a nun want to do back gainer with a flying squirrel toe touch. This swing would bring out the red in almost anybody. If you put a Yankee investment banker on this thing, he would be dipping Copenhagen before he hit the water. This was good country-ass fun.

In Mr. Sharp's defense, how was he to know where the line was? The line he crossed, although imperceptible to him, might as well have been carved in stone in our delinquent, silly little minds.

If you crossed the line, you paid the fine.

The gang was thirsty after perfecting the back flip/preacher seat combo at Big Creek, so we headed to the nearest water spigot, which doubled as our personal water fountain. Once we all had a little Buddha potbelly full of water, the door opened. No one ran. Why would we? We were drinking water, not smoking crack.

Mr. Sharp yelled for us to get off his grass, quit stealing his water, never step foot in his yard, and threw in a few harsh words that we didn't yet recognize. He broke cardinal rule number one: Respect the Weathington Boys. We were not above being yelled at, and the language didn't faze us, but to tell us what we could and could not do, especially during summer vacation, crossed the line. If you gave us respect and let us go about our day you could get away with a lot more. He may not have gotten the memo, but a smarter neighbor would have handled this differently.

★

For example, a few years later, Mike Lively was building a swanky new house on top of the hill. Mike wasn't stupid, and he knew if he wanted to build his home stress-free and hole-free, he needed to come see the Weathington Boys before he broke ground.

Mike cornered us in the field house after school one day. He pulled us aside, got up in our face, and told us if we damaged his house in any way he was coming down to beat our ass. Although Brian and I could have taken him at the time, Brian nodded and said it wouldn't be a problem. I was surprised by Brian's restraint; he was always more likely to hit you with a bat than I was.

"Why'd you let him punk us like that?"

"Mike runs Sewell's," Brian explained. Sewell's was a clothing manufacturer and the largest business in town. This was before the invention of Wal-Mart or China.

"So? He can still get his ass kicked!"

"It's three o'clock in the afternoon, Nathan."

I was still drawing a blank on why we were not wailing on him with a sock full of Jacks.

Brian was very calm — not one of his strong suits — which in turn calmed me down. He had obviously given this some thought and patiently took me through his reasoning. He knew we would see eye to eye or he would not have spoken for both of us in the first place. We rarely disagreed.

"Mike took off work, came down here in his suit, found us — a task the FBI has found challenging. This threat took planning. He knew before he called the city to get permission to build he had to come see us first."

"I follow you," I said.

"Respect," Brian declared.

Not only did we not trash his house, we made sure no would-be up-and-coming juvenile delinquents touched it either.

Back to that steamy, southern summer day. Mr. Sharp had not shown the appropriate amount of respect — not even close. After he finished his tirade, we all gave a weak apology and went about our day. We had plans to make.

Planning attacks was the most enjoyable part of my childhood. It was like a boardroom brainstorming meeting, but without shirts or anyone over age eleven. *PowerPoint* hadn't been invented, thank God. Digital documentation of these attacks would probably have gotten us five to ten.

Excitement and nervous energy was in the air, aided by the sweet tea and Lik-M-Aid. I loved these meetings even more than the actual attack. They were a chance for me to show off my creative side. I was much better at planning the correct way to shoot someone in the ass with a pellet gun, and Brian was much better at actually doing it. The preparation was elaborate. These meetings routinely lasted a few hours and included a variety of diagrams and sketches to cover positions, timing, supplies, and all other relevant details. I'm surprised the Pentagon didn't draft us straight out of elementary school. We met in our carport around a card table at about seven in the morning. No moss grew on us. We had things to do.

Brian and I were always first to the boardroom to cover classified topics before the rest of the gang arrived. We discussed things like what we would do if someone ratted on us or who we thought would get caught first if the fuzz was on our tail.

Then the rest of the gang arrived.

"What's the play?" Brian asked.

The new kids threw out ideas to try to impress us. Some weren't bad, but Brian shot them down with contempt.

"T.P. his house?"

"Been done," Brian said.

"Egg it?"

"More destructive, but boring," he said.

"Send him pizzas?"

Brian did not even acknowledge this idea.

"Fireworks?" I said.

"That's got legs."

Fireworks are illegal in the state of Georgia. But, about ten minutes down the road, conveniently just over the Alabama state line, stood Firework City, the Holy Grail of gunpowder. Not being able to drive did pose a small problem, but we quickly learned the art of hitchhiking. It's surprising and somehow heartening to recall a time when people willingly and unquestioningly picked up nine-year-old boys off the side of the highway and dropped them off at an explosives emporium. Brian and I did clean up pretty well when we wanted something, and with our dark skin we looked like a cross between a pre-teen Swedish boy

13

and a young Shaka Zulu. We were pure heat, just two cute innocent identical twin boys trying to get across the state line to the legal dynamite store. Our thumbs never broke a sweat and we were never gone long enough for our parents to miss us.

If you were a knowledgeable and therefore confident young firework buyer, you could walk out of Firework City essentially carrying a bundle of dynamite. They even threw in free Thunder Bombs with your purchase. This might seem crazy to kids today who carry Purell in their back pocket. Yes, you read correctly: we hitchhiked to the Wal-Mart of fireworks, shopped unsupervised, spent our own hard-earned money on explosive devices, and got free mini-sticks of dynamite for being such loyal customers. This was Bremen, Georgia, 1983. It was also time to take inventory.

"What kind of fireworks does everyone have left over?" asked Brian.

"Roman Candles," said the kid from Syria, who was new to fireworks, although very enthusiastic and showing huge potential.

"Bottle Rockets," piped the kid with the shiny, perfectly combed blond hair. This hair told the world his mom did not know he was with us. His fireworks were technically Whistlers, but I kept my mouth shut. It was an easy mistake to make, especially with hair like that. This is the same kid who would later get blasted with a fire extinguisher for counting down the remaining days of summer vacation.

"Snakes," whispered the preacher's son who'd recently moved to the neighborhood. He would later be forbidden by God to hang out with the Weathington Boys.

"Did you really just say 'Snakes'?" Brian asked. "That firework is so lame it's not even really a firework. Nathan, punch him."

Although he did deserve it, I didn't punch our new bible school friend. Instead, I did have an epiphany.

"Mammoth Smoke!" My voice rang with confidence and hoodlum victory.

"A smoke bomb is just as wimpy as my snakes," our Jesus freak friend retorted.

"This ain't a normal smoke bomb." Maybe I should have punched him.

There was nothing more embarrassing and revealing than a wannabe juvie not knowing his fireworks. This moron would not know the difference between a Ladyfinger and a Butterfinger. What a loser.

"Nathan, please educate our friend here on what a Mammoth Smoke is," Brian instructed.

Mr. Bible School thought about mouthing off, but saw Brian was carrying his bat and decided to take his natural position in the pecking order. Last.

To call a Mammoth Smoke a smoke bomb would have been like calling his momma big-boned.

"One Mammoth Smoke is the same as 10,000 of the things you call smoke bombs."

"So a Mammoth Smoke is the weapon. What's the plan?" Brian inquired.

"I know we're thinking carport or porch, the usual places, but I think the front door is the target," I responded.

"Huh? It will just blow away," Brian said.

"Well, there are actually two front doors, one main door and one air-tight storm door on the outside."

"I like it, go on."

"We put the smoke bomb—"

"You mean Mammoth Smoke."

"Excuse me. So we put the Mammoth Smoke between the doors and light it…"

"And ring the door bell!" our young Christian friend chimed in.

"You really should try to listen more and talk less. As I was saying, we light the Mammoth Smoke, and wait. It takes ten minutes to dump its full load. Then we ring it."

Brian said he was in; no one else had voting rights.

The plan was simple — no *PowerPoint* needed. The attack started the next day, broad daylight. We lit God's gift to smoke bombs and hit the bushes. The door was invisible within the first ten seconds. That storm door did its job; only small plumes of smoke escaped. The smoke became thick and looked like gravy. It appeared as if we would need a shovel to dig the smoke out of the door. Finally the hissing stopped. I darted up and rang the doorbell.

It took old Mr. Sharp a few minutes to get to the door. When he opened it, just as we had planned, the gravy of 10,000 smoke bombs was sucked into his face and his house. Spasmodic coughing and high pitched screaming ensued; he thought his house was on fire, a legitimate concern under the circumstances, and one that hadn't really crossed our minds. It was a nice bonus.

From our position, we could clearly see into his living room. A drunken chicken was crashing into furniture trying to piece together what the hell was going on. The smoke was thick, heavy, and starting to settle on the floor like a giant s'more.

It was time for us to move. Our policy for closing an attack was to get the hell out of Dodge before the neighbors or the cops showed up. Mr. Sharp was left gasping for air in his new marshmallow-themed living room as we sprinted through the woods. The gang fantasized about Mr. Sharp doing the Curly Shuffle on the floor for the next three days.

After that, we continued to drink from his faucet and use his yard as a thoroughfare to Big Creek without conflict. Maybe he now respected us, or maybe he was still in the hospital. Either way, we were back in charge.

The Great Wall
1983
9 years old

I

The weather forecast called for light snow, and the Weathington Boys forecasted you getting your ass kicked if you messed with our favorite precipitation. It rarely snowed in Bremen; when it did, it was up to the Weathington Boys to ensure every kid in a thirty-mile radius got a snow day. We had to get to work.

Before Al Gore caused global warming, it snowed at our house once every two or three years. We loved snow the way an Eskimo loves pineapple. All the kids in the town reminisced about The Big One. The Big One was a massive six-inch dump of snow, but as the years passed it got deeper and deeper. Now living in Canada, I realize how ridiculous we must have seemed to our northern neighbors. Grocery store chains prayed for a snow forecast. Bremen didn't actually need snow — just a chance of snow, and the entire town would lose their freakin' minds. Within hours of the news, you would only find bare shelves at Piggly Wiggly, a very highbrow local grocer, and the lines would stretch back to the meat counter. The good-ole-boys always loved the idea of having to live off the land like cavemen using just their wits, a fishing rod, and an AK-47 for survival. Even Brian and I couldn't help but nod our heads every time Hank Williams' *Country Boy Can Survive* came on the radio.

In our neighborhood lived an abundance of teachers, including my parents. The homes must have been affordable given the buying power of public school teachers in Georgia. More importantly, we had two principals and one superintendent living on our turf. Having what seemed like every one of our teachers as neighbors was a burden every day of our childhood, except this day.

The snow began falling on a Sunday night. It was light, but it stuck. Our neighborhood was rather hilly by local standards, which made it not only hard to get out of, but also a Mecca for would be sledders.

Brian and I were the picture of innocence as we looked out our window and talked about the exciting snow games we would play the next day. We already knew where the fort would go and who would be on what snowball team. My mom and dad were sitting in front of the fire reading and sipping hot chocolate.

Then Brian and I noticed our neighbor Mr. Doug Douglas, a principal of one of the local schools, driving around the neighborhood. He went by once and we did not pay attention. On the second trip around the neighborhood, I asked Brian if he thought Mr. Douglas was lost. On the third trip around, Brian jumped to attention. "What the hell?" We went downstairs and asked our parents what Mr. Douglas was up to. They explained he was trying to get rid of the snow on the roads to make it safe for us to all go to school the next day.

Get rid of the snow! Surely, I had heard incorrectly. Overcome with rage, my vision closed in and I almost blacked out, but before I did, Brian, with ice water in his veins, declared we were both tired and were going to bed. My parents eyed us as Brian led me away by my sleeve. Obviously, Brian was not tired, and besides the blacking out part, I was as keyed up as kangaroo on meth. I knew it was on.

Using all the cuss-words we knew at the time (damn and hell) to vent our anger toward Mr. Douglas, it was now time to get down to business. As far as we were concerned, the future of human civilization rested on our shoulders. There was no time to assemble the troops, and an emergency ten o'clock meeting was hard to pull off for nine year olds, even us. It didn't matter.

This job called for the real players: we didn't have time to baby-sit anyone who was out of shape or out of guts.

"We might not see snow like this again in our lifetime," Brian stated. "Doug will have ruined the best snow that has ever hit this town."

Brian and I hadn't mastered the art of moderation, a deficit that would plague us well into adulthood. In our demented little minds, it was either worth dying for or not worth doing at all.

A snow day was clearly worth dying for; still is, if you ask me.

Assessing our potential responses, we worked

through the usual violent attacks, but busting windows or egging someone's house didn't really solve the problem.

"Maybe we should attack his truck," I said.

"I agree, but I doubt we can pull it off with just the two of us."

"We need more snow."

"What about ice?"

Mom and Dad stayed up later than usual to enjoy the fire, or more likely because they were not buying Brian's "we're tired" act. However, as soon as they were finally asleep at eleven o'clock, we slipped out the back. Our idea would require at least 250 feet of garden hose, which meant we needed not only all the hoses from our house, but three neighbors' as well.

First thing first: Snuff out the snow hater. This was easily accomplished with our football-field-length hose. It wouldn't reach from our house, so we hooked it up to the hater's house. It was poetic justice, even if Brian and I hated poetry. Next, we watered every inch of his driveway. Two hours later, he had his very own ice rink. While we waited for Mr. Douglas' driveway to freeze, we hit the remaining big wigs in the neighborhood. It was hard work for two scrawny nine-year-olds to sneak the 100 pounds of water-filled hose through the dark, snow-covered woods. The round trip was about two miles. It was now two in the morning.

"Ok, all the big dogs have ice rinks for driveways. Do you think that's enough?" I asked.

"We need to block the street."

"How? We can't ice over the entire neighborhood. The sun will come up eventually, and Mom and Dad might be pissed if we aren't there for breakfast."

I was always the voice of reason in the gang, which is a bit of a scary thought. I was far from a mother hen: I just felt obligated to point out that dropping a cross tie on a car might kill someone. I never said we shouldn't do it; I just wanted to make sure we were all aware of what we were doing. As an aside, let's fast forward to our college years to find out what happened when the voice of reason left town.

Graduating early from college, I left Brian and the infamous Ray, whom I will formally introduce in a later chapter, without their voice of reason. Better said: Brian and Ray took two extra years to graduate. It was touch-and-go if they were going to make it out of there alive and without a jailhouse tattoo. They like to paint me as a prude, and I guess I am compared to them, but so is Charles Manson. Although they give me a hard time, I know they are thankful for my valuable counseling over the years. For the record, I have never told them they should not do something. I was smart enough to phrase it another way.

"I'm not trying to tell you two how to live your lives, but we're over 18, and this stunt is a minimum of five years in real ass-rape level prison. Do you think it's worth it?"

"Maybe not when you put it that way. Good point, Nate," Brian or Ray would say. It should be mentioned that Brian and Ray were the only ones who called me Nate; when others did I usually corrected them. Although it was never addressed, it felt forced, like one of my son's slack-jawed schoolmates calling me 'Dad.'

Unfortunately, I can't comment much on those college years. Although damn entertaining, there might be

some statute of limitation issues, and I can't afford a law-
yer at this time. The general book-buying public also might
not see the humor in an old-school B&E, beating up cops,
racketeering, slapping around and robbing a boy band, or
breaking someone's ass in half if they mess with Willie
Nelson. Well, maybe the boy band part. I'll put that in the
next book.

★

Back to saving civilization — and our snow day.

"We have to block the street!" Brian said again,
sharply.

Urgency was setting in; we were getting panicky and
starting to snap at each other. Had we failed at our mission? Were all the kids going to have to go to school the
next day because of our ineptness? Had we tarnished our
good name?

"We have to do it. We have no choice," I said.

"Well, they all have to come out the same road,"
Brian contemplated.

"They all go up the hill in front of the house," I
responded.

"True. I wish we could ice over the entire hill or make
it too thick to drive over."

"It's not cold enough for that many layers."

"But we could shovel it all from the neighborhood
and put it in one spot."

Brian and I instantly knew this was our only hope.
We picked up two five-gallon buckets and two shovels from
the shed. Discussing it further was a waste of time.

There was not a single complaint issued during the

next four hours of hard labor. It was below freezing and we were in short sleeves, but we didn't have the luxury of time to dress ourselves properly. Our people needed us: no kid would be left behind. The snow might have been a half-inch deep in the thickest spot. We scraped every flake we could find and put it in buckets that we ran up the hill and placed on the Bremen version of the Great Wall. We worked like the slaves on the pyramids — minus the heat, daylight, and repetitive whipping.

Three hours later at around five in the morning, it looked as if it had snowed only in a five foot tall, 25-foot wide section of wall barricading the road. We shaped and packed it with pride. Our hands were ice themselves, but the warmth of delinquency kept us going. Once we had a rough design in place, it was still just snow, and a pickup truck could bust through.

"I'm starting to feel good about this," Brian said.

"Me too."

"We need to ice it."

"Obviously."

The wall ran between two homes. We split our hoses and ran two lines. The wall was soaked for the remainder of the night. As the sun came up, we replaced all hoses and tools and slid back into bed. We had been there barely long enough to warm up when my mom called us down for yet another amazing breakfast.

Our mom served us a hot breakfast every day of our lives. Sometimes I think the only thing that kept us out of the Pen was my mom's homemade biscuits. I'm hoping the same strategy works on my boys.

We woke up groggy, but excited. My dad commented that we still looked tired, but Mom's biscuits were soon the center of attention, and my dad went about sketching another brilliant football play on his napkin.

"I know you don't want to go school today," my dad said. "But it doesn't look like there is much snow on the ground. Sorry, boys."

"There goes Doug," my mom said.

"Good luck," Brian mumbled with a biscuit in his mouth.

I pretended to choke as I got my laughter under control.

"Doug's back fast; it must not be clear," Mom said.

"That's weird; Tim hasn't made it out either."

At this point, we started packing in the biscuits; we had a big day ahead of us.

Slowly, everyone started to come out of their homes to see what exactly was going on. Since there was zero snow or ice on the road, people were wondering why everyone who left for work or school promptly came back. Simultaneously, all neighborhood eyes fell on the large white wall in the middle of the black asphalt. It became the focus of conversation. Brian and I feigned confusion as we asked what was going on. Many of the neighbors flocked to the wall like those old farts in *Cocoon*. They touched it, kicked at it, and stood on it. Unless someone had a backhoe and five sticks of dynamite, it was not moving.

It worked much better than we had planned. It was so hard it did not even feel like ice. It was more like a cold block of granite. The wall also had an ice slick downstream from the leftover water; a nice touch that slowed down would-be rammers. I can only imagine what it feels like for a woman to bring life onto this planet, but I'm pretty sure it would pale in comparison to the pride, excitement, and overwhelming joy Brian and I felt toward that wall.

Everyone was confused about where the wall came from, including my mom and dad. My dad was actually confused, but this was Mom's normal routine. Anytime something was amiss, she always knew who did it, but would go along with the shock and confusion of the rest of the pack.

I swear she could have passed a lie detector test; the woman is a genius. She was a silent partner in our escapades in some respects. Just like us, she would never rat out a friend, and her friends in this case were her two delinquent sons. Her voice would not crack or stutter, and she had a tight poker face only Brian and I could read. Her face would appear warmer to the two of us, despite the fact her expression was unchanged to the general public. She always thought of us as clever, not mischievous, and enjoyed our freedom as much as we did. Now I don't want to give the impression my mom was a pushover. She would not tolerate us being disrespectful in any way, and we always did as we were told.

She had not specifically said not to barricade the neighborhood.

So why in the world did she allow us to run feral, destroying everything in our path? She loved us, but all moms love their kids.

Unlike every other mom in town, I now know that we highly entertained her. She found the merit badge, prom king, bible freak, and piano-playing choirboys boring. And if we were anything, it wasn't boring. I know she had to keep a straight face and remain stern when she disciplined us. However, how mad could she realistically be at two boys industrious enough to shut down the entire school system, thus allowing her a well-deserved day off?

Our mom always protected us; or maybe she was protecting herself. Either way, it worked to our advantage.

Brian and I returned home to listen for the school closures on the radio. They read them off one by one. They finished by naming Bremen City Schools. Just as we had planned, if the school VIPs could not make it in, the little people would be free. Brian gave me a very subtle nod. Mission accomplished.

My mom entered the house in near hysterics. She already had tears in her eyes from laughing.

"You two..." she stopped as if she were about to say something very profound.

"Are quite unbelievable."

II.

Although we'd been awake for 27 hours, the day wasn't over yet. We were just getting warmed up. The overly aggressive snowball fight was first, followed by the most dangerous sledding you could possibly imagine. We didn't have the luxury of a snow-blanketed road like our spoiled Yankee and Canadian neighbors: some fancy maneuvering was necessary if you wanted to avoid road rash (the snow farming for the Great Wall had left large bare patches of asphalt). Sparks lit up the road behind our sleds in an impressive light show.

Next was a ten-person flat-bottom boat ride down the hill. Just for your information: The momentum of a flat-bottom boat with ten guys — and your mom — going down a steep, ice-glazed hill is far greater than the static force of a maroon 4x4 mailbox post, standard issue as per the bylaws of our posh neighborhood. Said boat will snap it off like a toothpick.

Although it had been an action-packed night and day, we still had one more attack left. Like pint-sized generals at the Battle of Fort Sumter, we arranged our elementary school troops in positions on either side of the Wall and distributed every last snowball that could be mustered.

The Great Wall was as we'd left it early that morning. But now a Lincoln Town Car, a massive car with plenty of muscle under the hood, approached the Wall.

The driver got out, sized up the obstacle with disdain and figured she could bust through. She had a bitter scowl on her face, as hard as the wall, as she climbed once again behind the wheel of her Lincoln leviathan.

She backed up about a hundred feet and got a running start. Her speed was impressive, almost scary. Brian and I watched in mute fascination as the Lincoln hit the Wall straight on. The Wall won. It did not even flake. The Lincoln crumpled like an accordion. The woman jumped out of the car, crying and screaming in her Sunday best.

It was go time. Every boy simultaneously jumped from his hiding spot in the snowball version of D-Day. She looked like Snow White trying to fend off those seven horny midgets. Even the limp-wristed, unathletic kids were lighting her up.

Brian and I both had cannons for arms, and he could thread the needle. Brian was so skilled at throwing that he never just tried to hit you, he tried for a specific part of you. It was a headshot or nothing. If I knew him, he was aiming for the face as well: The back of the head just did not splat the same. The beauty of the mass attack is no one knows who actually threw the kill shot, except the person who threw it, or his twin brother, in this case. Brian made his target on the second throw.

Luckily it was not a battle-grade snowball. It was a gentle yet effective splat that covered most of her face. To say she was crying would be an understatement. Wailing would be more appropriate.

Brian and I knew this was the climax of a long, well-earned day off from school. Before all hell broke loose, we slid out the back and were home in time for dinner. Mom's vegetable soup was a mainstay on snow days. This, along with the homemade southern cornbread that probably had more lard than corn in it, sent us straight into a food coma.

Brian and I both slept for twelve hard hours. Sacrifices sometimes must be made for the betterment of society. We were the juvenile suburban version of Robin Hood, and the snow-deprived kids of rural Georgia were the beneficiaries.

The Great Wall lasted for weeks. Eventually, once it softened, neighbors used picks and shovels to clear off one lane for traffic. Remnants of ice were still on the road a month later, when we were back in our cutoffs.

Brian and that Damn Bat

PART I

1983

9 years old

Brian never killed anyone with his bat. To this day, it's almost impossible for me to talk or write about Brian's bat without laughing. He was a fearless warrior, but instead of being thrown into a battlefield, he was thrown into some of the weirdest situations with some strange country-ass people. I still believe we were extremely normal kids; we were just continually confronted with odd circumstances. It was eat or be eaten: Bremen was our Serengeti, and no one was stealing our dead gazelle.

In our neighborhood, sports were played year-round: football, basketball, and baseball mostly. No one owned a video game, and if they did, they didn't play it or admit to playing it in public. Baseball games would last into the night. This was good, harmless fun, as long as everyone left us alone.

There wasn't a real ball diamond around, so we used an odd-shaped, extremely-sloped vacant lot in our neighborhood. A backstop kept the balls from going down the hill, and we cut down a few trees to help clear the outfield, a move that didn't make the landowner very happy. A homerun was over the road and into the yard of a strange man.

The first neighbor we ran into in the outfield, whom I will refer to as Mr. Jackass, decided a baseball landing in his yard was unacceptable. It was not like we were hitting them through his windows, or at least not at the time. He couldn't leave well enough alone, though, and one day as we were wrapping up the game he came to scold us. It was a brief talk about how we were by-no-means-to-hit-a-baseball-in-his-yard-ever-again. We didn't pay him much attention. Being new to the neighborhood, he was about to get a quick education in who actually ran the joint.

One sunny afternoon soon afterward we were in the fifth inning, and he stood in his yard with his hands on his hips waiting for a ball to hit his lovely grass. Everyone hit to right field or away from his yard, until Brian came up.

He approached the plate with the Little League equivalent of Robert Redford's Wonderboy bat in *The Natural*. Excalibur was a 30-inch silver Easton Speed Demon special. It was much shinier than when it came off the shelf. He was continually hitting rocks, trees, and baseballs, and was about to expand this list to include a couple of grown men. All this wear and tear kept it continually shaved down to the bare aluminum.

I was pitching. As I looked up to see who was at bat I saw Brian grinning as if he had stolen the prize out of our box of Cookie Crisp — which he was known to do from time to time. Once again, I knew it was on.

32

I lobbed one in there like a cantaloupe — might as well have some fun. Brian drilled a line drive right at his head. Mr. Jackass side-stepped it at the last second, and then ran to get the ball. He sprinted over to us and proceeded to threaten each one of us individually.

"Ya lookin' for trouble thar, boy?" he said to our shortstop as he poked him in the chest. As Mr. Jackass was walking over to our first baseman, the shortstop looked to me for help, I was frozen.

"That's my yerd, not yer damn outfield," he said as he gently shoved our first baseman.

In retrospect, I now realize how completely ridiculous this man's behavior was. Now as a "grown man" myself, I can't picture being drunk enough, high enough, or angry enough to pick a fight with a group of nine-year-olds.

I was a bit taken off guard and must admit I was a bit scared. This was the first time anyone had directly taken us on; I was not sure how we would handle the situation. Everyone knew we should do something, but we all hesitated.

We were in jeopardy of losing all the power we had accumulated at this point in our childhoods. This could have been the fork in the road that led us towards a normal childhood — we needed someone to lead us.

Mr. Jackass then looked Brian right in the eye and said, "You got a problem thar, big boy?"

Brian never broke eye contact, although he was no longer grinning. He picked up his bat, grabbed his prepubescent manhood and sneered, "I got your 'big boy' right here," and started walking directly at Mr. Jackass — on his toes, like a boxer. Mr. Jackass had not considered the possibility of a counter-offensive; I hadn't either for that matter.

I noticed Mr. Jackass was looking a bit shocked, though at this point not scared, by one nine year old with a bat. He should have been.

I realized then Brian was right. Who was this weirdo coming over to threaten us and tell us we could no longer play baseball? As the man prepared for battle against his nine-year-old foe, I decided if he was going to kill Brian, he was going to have to whoop two nine-year-old asses that day. I was not alone. Without a word spoken, we were all ready to fight to the death.

Whether out of peer pressure or loyalty to the group, every other kid simultaneously crept in and around Mr. Jackass. We were all wolves and the silent attack signal had been given. Despite his best efforts to hide it, our prey's face was lathered with panic as he began looking around for an escape route. Everyone held their positions. I was surprised at Brian's behavior, but utterly shocked by the straight kids' performance. At the end of the day, every boy received his unofficial badass merit badge, even the preacher's son.

We shoved Mr. Jackass from one side of the circle to the other as he tried to focus on the eight mini-thugs who had him cornered. This was not how he originally saw this playing out; I'm sure he'd already rehearsed the script where he tells his ugly wife how he took care of business. Instead, he was ordered to get the hell off our baseball field and go home, which he did. What else could he do? If he stayed there, he was going to get hurt, and it would have been weird for him to explain to our parents how their nine-year-old sons had threatened him. He was ours.

Over the next several months, we would torment him with rocks in his gutters, gas tanks, and windows.

He moved within a year.

Brian and that Damn Bat

PART II

1983

10 years old

The first time we came face to face with the second man living in our outfield, he was firing a rifle with his trained attack dog at his side, while Brian tried to kill him with his bat. Our relationship was off to a rough start.

I had been pitching to Brian, and in the background I heard growling and gunshots; this being rural Georgia I barely paid it any attention; these noises were the soundtrack to our childhood. Brian had let two crappy pitches go by with a gentlemanly show of patience. As I was getting ready to pitch again, he looked over my head into the outfield, which happened to now be Mr. Sketchball's yard. Brian's face seemed pale, and his eyes and jaw were both locked rigidly in place.

He never said one word. With his trusty Easton in

hand, he took off in a full sprint toward the outfield. I was completely confused. I thought he was about to kill someone in the outfield at first, but he ran by our much-relieved left fielder and closed in fast on the man. My stomach sank; I knew something heavy was about to go down.

Still unclear on what exactly that was, I knew it was serious so I ran after Brian. As I closed in, I put together the incident like a mini Magnum P.I. with a duck-tailed mullet instead of a mustache:

Our first pet was Fluffy, a battleship gray feline. We loved Fluffy; she was an excellent hunter and came to all our baseball games. On this occasion, for whatever reason, Mr. Sketchball had released his pit bull on Fluffy to kill her. He then was following up the attack with shots from his .22-caliber rifle.

In case you live above the Mason-Dixon Line or in the suburbs, a .22 is the smallest rifle on the market. It's an extremely dangerous gun as people underestimate its power. This type of gun can kill deer — something Brian and I can attest to — or people, and this idiot was firing like a drunken Sarah Palin into our outfield. My sister says he was a gangster, but I can't confirm that.

A normal human being would have avoided this shitshow like herpes — not Brian. It was the first time I had ever seen Brian truly mad. His eyes were wide as saucers and he was looking for blood. Brian's body went rigid as he poised to strike at the first opportunity. The previous attack on Mr. Jackass was nothing compared to this. Brian was a gladiator: he didn't hesitate against a man firing a gun while his attack dog frothed at his side.

As I did have the de facto responsibility of being the rational one in the group, I realized this situation had really gotten out of hand. Guns, bats, attack dogs — we needed Dad.

I sprinted from the scene feeling as if I was abandoning Brian, but at the same time I knew we needed reinforcements. Looking back, I'm impressed with my clear reasoning under what others might call a stressful situation. In our entire lives Brian and I only asked our parents for help twice; this marked the first. The second time, we were on the verge of burning down the entire town — clearly another story.

Both our parents knew I wouldn't ask for help unless some real shit was going down. They were both relaxing on the deck when I arrived.

"Mr. Sketchball has a gun and Brian's after him with a bat!" I yelled.

"Where?" my dad replied with a very serious look on his face.

"The baseball field."

My dad was on his feet in a fast and fluid motion, similar to the ones his players did during warm-ups. His 'little bastard' dropped from his hand without a second thought. (A little bastard is a small 7 oz bottle of beer, a.k.a. a Pony.)

We all three sprinted the hill. When we arrived, Brian had landed a few, but this was not enough to mellow the wild animal look in his eye.

Mom pulled Brian aside and calmed him down. While hugging him, she told him it was over and that everything was going to be okay. I stuck close to Dad. My dad, Coach Weathington as he was better known, looked like he was born in a weight room and fed nothing but cornbread his entire life. He was solid and had the athleticism and army training to make other men insecure. His presence alone tended to diffuse a situation.

In addition, my dad was an incredibly nice and polite man. He never hit us, which is saying a lot. Even the Dalai Lama would have been hard-pressed not to switch our ass at some point. He walked up to Mr. Sketchball, now rubbing the bruises on his shins, and simply requested the gun, which was dutifully relinquished. Next, my dad calmly directed the man to put his attack dog away, an order promptly obeyed.

We held back the tears, but we were very upset about Fluffy. Shot in the eye and now 200 feet up a tree, my parents weren't finished yet; my dad went straight to the neighbors and borrowed a giant extendable ladder used for climbing telephone poles. It did not reach Fluffy. Although my dad was jacked, he was built more for hauling trees than climbing them. After reaching the top of the ladder, he shimmied up the pine tree, risking his life for a cat. Now I was scared not only for Fluffy but also for my dad — my mom assured me that nothing bad was going to happen, although her facial expression said otherwise. Personally, I do not know if I would swerve for a cat. Well, only Fluffy.

At this point, Mr. Sketchball yelled up for my dad to be careful in a slightly rude tone.

"Well I wouldn't be up this damn tree if it wasn't for your stupid ass," my dad yelled down.

I then realized that all the kids in the neighborhood were huddled steps away from the mayhem. I had not even noticed them. They all smiled as Mr. Sketchball tucked into his house with his tail between his legs, never to return. He never made eye contact with us again. My parents took

Fluffy to the vet, which is kind of like taking a disposable camera in for repairs. However, they loved us.

We tortured that poor man as if he were our own personal POW. Nothing was off limits: B&E, eggs, sugar in the gas tank, busted windows, keyed car, bottle rockets, burnt grass, busted mailbox, and a good ole power bird every time he drove by the baseball field.

He also moved out after less than a year as the property value in our outfield continued to plummet.

Jesus Saves ...
Most of the Time
1982 TO 1988
8 to 14 years old

EASTER EGG LEGENDS

Only God could save the Weathington Boys, or so the theory went. Bremen, Georgia, is the buckle of the Bible Belt, so the local evangelical Christians pressured my mom to bring Jesus into the lives of her two hellions. It was as awkward and ill-acted as Michael Jackson and Lisa Marie's televised kiss.

Our church was fairly conservative by local standards, which I guess only means there were no snakes, talking in tongues, or healing of the cripple in front of a televised audience. Had there been snakes, Brian and I might have stuck around a bit longer.

It's tough to know if you should expect human sacrifices, exorcisms, or orgies inside a church simply by

41

examining the cracks in the stucco or rips in the tent. A general rule of thumb is to avoid the churches with the longest names. We attended the Bremen First United Methodist Church, not a long name comparatively. This name makes sense: It was located in Bremen, it was a Methodist Church, and the words First and United are general fillers when it comes to naming places of worship. I have yet to see a second or third version of a specific sect — but I can't blame them — who would want to advertise that they were God's second and third chosen place of worship in a small rural town. Church names grow from feuds. Here's how the nomenclature works: Deacon Smith sleeps with Deacon Jones' wife. Deacon Jones punches Deacon Smith in the dick. Deacon Smith now takes Deacon Jones' wife and splinters off from the original church, yet wants to leverage the existing church brand. He names his new church the Bremen First United Deliverance Ministries Methodist Church. A few years later, someone screws Deacon Smith's wife, a.k.a. Deacon Jones' ex-wife, and now you have the Bremen First United Evangelical Deliverance Ministries Methodist Church.

The Church Years were not a total loss; we did add the next official vote-casting member to our duo. We met Ashley during our first religious heist. Those gullible Christian folks always assumed everyone in church was moral or wanted to be, which made them easy prey. And naïve.

Brian and I were less than interested in almost everything that happened at church. The skits, the praying, the bible reading, it was all about as interesting as hearing about the "crazy" dream your friend had the night before. Spring was in the air and Easter was upon us. I'm still a little bit confused by the connection between Easter's Christ rising from the grave story and how it relates to chocolate mammals laying eggs. The church was putting on an Easter egg hunt. Chasing around colored eggs with no street value did not excite us. However, Easter is the time of miracles.

The bible school teacher informed us there would be a prize for the person who found the most eggs — seven silver dollars. Jesus just got interesting. Money was on the line, and there was nothing like a little juice to get our attention. Maybe this church thing was not so bad after all.

It only took a brief glance between us to know that we were going to win those silver dollars. These amateur egg hunters were about to get their asses handed to them.

The starting gun fired. We took off and were snatching eggs from all over. We were faster, better coordinated, and were willing to get a little dirty if need be. Both our baskets appeared to have the most eggs in them. I had 15 and Brian 16. As we were heading to the judging table, we heard Matthew Miller yell out he had 18.

No problem there, we just moved to phase two of the plan. I dumped ten of my eggs into Brian's basket and he called, "I have 26." We collected our prize, Brian got four and I got three of the silver dollars. Our payroll rationale should be obvious.

I know it seems completely immoral to cheat at an Easter egg hunt. However, it could be argued that cheating made more sense than chocolate bunnies mixed with bloody crosses and monetary prizes for finding hidden eggs in bushes in the first place.

A few kids saw what we had done, but didn't dare cross us. They were horrified by our sin, yet too chicken-shit to say anything about it. But one kid did have the guts to say something — Ashley.

Ashley walked up and asked us if we had indeed cheated at an Easter egg hunt to win seven silver dollars. Brian, sensing we were being challenged, glared him down and said, "Yep. Do you have a problem with that?"

"Hell no, that's brilliant. I just wish I'd thought of it," Ashley replied.

Two miracles occurred that Easter: We won loot and a friend at church. We were best friends soon after. Ashley liked to hunt and fish every waking second, the same as we did. But far and away his best quality was his mouth.

Ashley Sanders ran his mouth more than any human being we knew. He incessantly made fun of everyone. No one was off-limits — moms, dogs, sisters, your dad, religious figures; he had a rip on all of them. Unfortunately, this type of humor comes at a price; it's only a matter of time before you misjudge your audience and might have to fight your way out of a cocktail party.

I am now 40 years old, and every one of my friends still uses the term "pulling an Ashley." Some people use the phrase and don't even know Ashley.

The saying comes from one of Ashley's first jobs. On his first day of work, he met his boss in the Piggly Wiggly parking lot. They were pulling away in the truck when a very large woman crossed their path. Trying to impress the boss with his quick wit, Ashley yelled, "Look out for her boss! She'll total your truck."

Silence.

Then: "That's my wife."

More silence.

His gorilla-like wife then joined them in the cab of the truck. Keep in mind this was in the early eighties: No crew cabs back then. They sat shoulder to shoulder for the one-hour drive to the worksite. If you do not incessantly make fun of everyone you come in contact with, you may never "pull an Ashley." However, you are also probably a Yankee and not very funny.

STAFF OF RA

A square peg will not fit in a round hole no matter how hard you bang it. Since we were obviously not connecting with God the way we were supposed to, the church executives decided to make us acolytes. An acolyte is a watered down version of an altar boy. It's a good thing too; if someone had tried to touch our junk, we would have stuck them with a frog gig.

Like every other thing we'd been assigned at church, this was beyond dull. The one saving grace was that every Sunday acolytes got to walk to the front of the church and light the candles with a small torch. Our hard-wired propensity toward all things fire was not discovered until this point in our childhood.

Everyone got to carry the torch once, and each acolyte controlled the length of his flame. A wager had to be made, and everyone threw in two dollars. The kid who walked down the aisle with the largest torch would win $14.

Normally, the flame should be the size of a candle's. I had to give the straight kids credit; they weren't afraid to step it up a notch. The flame went from its customary one-inch size to about four inches during the first four Sundays. There were three left. I was next.

I bumped it up to a half a foot. People in the

congregation finally noticed, but I played dumb. I told them I didn't realize that I'd melted the candles I was assigned to light with my torch. Brian was next. I expected Brian to enter ready to kickoff the next Olympics, but he only put out enough to win — a mere seven inches.

The following Sunday, Ashley was up. Ashley's parents didn't find delinquency nearly as entertaining as my mom did, so the stakes were higher. Ashley wanted the title outright and there was only one way to take it — use the entire wick. Right before his entry, when no one was watching, he extended the wick to its full two feet.

It took a few seconds to fully ignite, but by the time he reached our pew, Brian tasted defeat. Brian and I smiled and nodded in admiration. Ashley grinned all the way to the front as black smoke billowed to the ceiling from his small town Staff of Ra. I glanced over at Ashley's mom, who had her face buried in her hands; she didn't think it was half as funny as we did. Ashley then proceeded to light his two assigned candles. The next time you have a dinner party, dip your broom in gasoline and then try lighting the candles with it. Those candles looked like a beaver had chewed them off in the middle with a flamethrower.

Brian and I had been beaten, and defeat had never been sweeter.

ELECTROCUTING THE PREACHER

To hell with the Sabbath, Sunday was for fishing. Church was grueling monotony. Every second in Church was one less second fishing. An hour for Church was long enough, but if you wanted to go into O.T., we would need to charge you time and a half.

Every Sunday after our preacher finished his canned sermon, he would stroll to the back of the church and start a receiving line. I guess he thought we wanted to stand in line for 30 minutes just to be close to His Holiness. Whatever the point of it, he was holding us up and Brian was pissed.

The next Sunday, Brian and I quickly broke in line to get it over with. Brian had something else in store for Mr. Rev; this was the only joke Brian never let me in on. He thought it would be funnier that way and he was right. The Rev knew about us but apparently thought his brilliant sermons were turning us around.

He reached out to shake Brian's hand in that I-am-so-much-more-important-than-you-are kind of way. Hidden in Brian's hand was a shocker. I don't think they sell these anymore. The local convenience store carried a rack of practical jokes such as this very thing, as well as stink bombs and itching powder. That store knew us intimately.

Brian reached for his hand and gave him a nice jolt. The preacher was caught off guard. I am pretty sure this was the first time someone had electrocuted him in the sanctity of his house of worship. He jerked his hand back and mumbled, "You little sh...." But he did not say it. He almost did, but not quite, and we have often pondered the fallout had he not restrained himself.

Damn, how I wished I'd thought of the buzzer. On the way home we told Mom; she thought it was hilarious. At least one person got us.

BARF-O-RAMA

Now forever excused from acolyte duty and the receiving line, we set our sights on communion. I did like the idea of taking a small snack break during the service; but the seriousness of the event combined with the small portions was destined to cause problems.

Brian, Ashley, and I were kneeling, which in itself is embarrassing, but the fact that you had to do it in front of everyone made me feel like the lone stripper in Mayberry — all eyes were upon us. All the other kids our age surrounded us. It warmed the hearts of the well-meaning Christian parents to see all of us in perfect harmony with Jesus Christ Our Lord. A PhD in sociology should not have been necessary to see the flaws of this social engineering. I am not sure how it started, but someone got the giggles.

Our family is not normal. You will get a gold star if you can make someone laugh until they spit food or blow milk out their nose. When someone started to get the giggles, we would move in for the kill with chants, jokes, and poking.

This behavior unfortunately made its way to the altar during this particular day of worship. I can't remember who, how, or what started it, but out of the corner of my eye I saw someone next to Brian struggling to keep his bread and grape juice in his mouth. The three of us closed in like a televangelist to an offering plate and tried to get everyone to spit up their grape juice. Unfortunately, we also had Welch's Blood of Christ in our mouths, so it kind of backfired.

I had to close my eyes and tense up my entire body to keep the blood of Jesus from spraying all over the pulpit. My mom commented afterwards that, although I didn't spit out my juice or laugh aloud, I was just as guilty as Brian and Ashley due to the redness of my ears. I argued my case, but I knew she was right. Moms know their sons in a way dads can't. My wife is like a Jedi Master; she can tell how many cookies my oldest son will steal even before they're baked.

Once the floodgates opened, all hell broke loose. One of the rookie kids in the laugh-until-you-puke game caved first. He blew out a fine mist of grape juice onto the preacher's white robe. This set everybody off. Even Brian, who was a seasoned vet at the game, lost his juice once he saw the shrapnel. It was kind of like shooting someone only to have the bullet ricochet back and kill you.

Brian spat a full shot glass of grape juice on the holy robes. I hoped they had Holy Bleach in the back. Once Brian blew juice, it was inevitable that Ashley would as well. Ashley's juice was a millisecond behind Brian's.

Mr. Preach finished serving the rest of the people and then had to get up in front of the congregation and give his sermon with two large grape juice splats close to his crotch, kind of like a Scarlet Letter for pedofiles.

Jesus never asked us to brunch again.

SERIOUSLY? CHOIR?

With communion, the receiving line, and acolyting decidedly and permanently off-limits, what part of "lock the Weathington Boys in a room and make them sing hymns" seemed like a logical idea? Maybe they were just trying to come up with a reason to use a big word like "juxtaposition" to impress the congregation.

My mom had dropped us off for the first choir practice and was heading across town to work. We were a few minutes in and mouthing the B, I, B, L, E song as we snuck out the back.

Once outside, we heard a train coming. It was going slow. Perfect. Although it violated our parole at the time — which you'll read about later — it was too hard to pass up. We jumped the train and rode it across town and almost beat my mom back to work. Once we were close to my mom's school, we abandoned ship. I don't think we ever told my mom how we actually got there so fast; we didn't want her to worry.

We all knew that was the end of choir.

JACKIE ROBINSON

My best friend at the time was Jerome Parham, more affectionately called Biscuit. He had moved to Bremen from the rough side of Atlanta and fit in about as well as we did.

The first time I met Biscuit we were suspended from school for eating our class's baked goodies in Home Ec. A lovely lady, our teacher was far from scary, and when she threatened to paddle the two us, Biscuit erupted into laughter with me in tow.

Biscuit was just like us in every way but one, and this one difference led to some odd situations. It never really crossed our minds, but we were white and Biscuit was black. If it makes you feel more educated, feel free to call us Caucasians and African Americans, or if there are newer politically-correct racial categories, you may use those as well.

Biscuit loved to point out the racist slang that we unknowingly used as part of our inherited vocabulary. Just to avoid an ass-beating from my mom as an adult,

I would like to emphatically state this was not inherited from my family, but from other mo-rods around town. We were always quite horrified and embarrassed when Biscuit would break down a word like niggerrig phonetically.

On one occasion, someone knowingly dropped the N-bomb in reference to Biscuit. Given the plethora of single-wides around, Biscuit looked nervous. She pulled a switchblade (yes, it was a girl). Knowing that she had a larger brother nearby, Biscuit was rightfully scared, but not for long.

"Oh really. I got something for you, Bitch," our buddy Ray piped in as he reached behind the seat of his dad's truck.

Ray pulled out a hog-leg .357 Magnum and pointed it at the girl's forehead.

"I'm sorry, I couldn't hear ya," Ray said as the color drained out of the girl's face. She tried to apologize, but no words came out. Brian insisted she pissed herself, but it was too dark to tell. Although the gun was loaded, she didn't understand that the stiff hammer had to be cocked to actually shoot her — she wasn't in that much danger.

Although skin tone is merely an aesthetic quality, the church you attend based on such a characteristic is not. There is a distinct difference between black and white churches. Some might say it is like night and day. Having attended both black and white churches, I can tell you that the paler version is like watching paint peel while the other is not. But while black churches are more fun, they routinely run into extra innings. So both have their drawbacks.

By the way, if you find this language racist it's because you're aroused by compost or live in Vermont and have no idea if you're racist or not and would love nothing more than to view all southerners as ignorant hillbillies.

"No church, no fishing," Mom told Ray, Brian, Biscuit, and me.

"Come on."

"I'm not budging on this. No church, no fishing."

We didn't have much choice and went upstairs to get ready. Brian and I were finding some extra clothes for our guests when Biscuit spoke up.

"Any black guys at yer chuch?"

"I don't think so, now that you mention it."

Biscuit's eyes lit up.

"Has a black man ever been to yer chuch?"

Brian and I shrugged; we'd only seen honkies since our arrival. Biscuit ushered us to the stairs to ask my parents.

"I don't think so," Mom whispered embarrassed.

Biscuit came leaping down the stairs, grinning from ear to ear.

"I'm sorry Biscuit, you don't have to go," my mom said, trying to give him an out.

"Oh, I'm going. Can we stop by my house on the way?"

We drove Biscuit to his house at the end of a dusty road. After five minutes inside, a phoenix came strutting through the dust dressed in a shiny purple suit. His suit was topped off with a tie and pocket square, both a crisp white. This thing snapped. Having only shopped at the white boy clothing stores we'd never seen a purple suit. Prince would have been proud.

"Nice suit," Mom said matter-of-factly.

"Thank you, Mrs. Weathington." Biscuit always had the best manners of the four of us.

We strolled and Biscuit strutted into church. He was eating it up, shaking hands, telling jokes, and doing anything in his power to make the stodgy old white ladies uncomfortable. Once he was done running for mayor on the front steps, Brian and I ushered our new celebrity friend to our seats in the back of the church.

"I ain't sittin' in the back of this chuch," Biscuit said with a toothy smile as if he were Rosa Parks.

He then began a slow meandering strut all the way to the front of the church. He was mindful to nod, point, and hug as many white girls and women as he was allowed. All four of us finally reached the front pew after what seemed like thirty minutes.

"Are you happy now?" I asked.

"You're like Jackie Robinson," Ray said from the other side.

Even funnier to Brian and me was that Ray stuck out about as bad as Biscuit. He just didn't know it.

Biscuit sang his ass off. He would have been a deacon, but like us just couldn't get by the monotony.

As we approached the end of the Church Years, God still had one last miracle to throw our way.

MOTHERFUCKER, DICK, PUSSY, SNOT, AND SHIT. GOOD NIGHT!

Eddie Murphy's movie *Raw* was the first R-rated movie I ever watched. It started as a routine Youth Group fieldtrip to the movie theatre, then Eddie showed up on screen and pummeled our Christian ears with F-bombs. God bless that brilliant, hilarious man.

The youth group took up two complete rows in the theater. Our eyes were glued to the screen from the first moment Eddie said Fuck, which — if you haven't seen it — is quite early in the movie. Our vocabulary was rapidly elevated to that of drunken sailors looking for prostitutes in Thailand. We not only learned new cuss words, but also how to use them properly in day-to-day conversations.

The next hour and a half was pure bliss. I hung on every word that came out of Eddie's filthy mouth and had to pinch myself to remember to breathe. We went in boys and came out men. I think I grew some pubic hair while in there. Brian, Ashley and I imitated Eddie the entire bus ride home. We didn't own two-piece purple leather suits, but we sure as hell could grab our nuts and yell at fellow passengers. As I write this, I find it amusing that both Eddie and Biscuit wore purple suits.

Eddie was fresh on our minds when we arrived home at nine o'clock. We never cussed in front of our parents, so I assume they heard us talking about the movie in general. My mom promptly figured out where we had been.

"You watched *Raw!*" she yelled.

"Yes ma'am," we mumbled.

"How did you get in?"

"We walked in with everyone else," I said confused.

"Everyone from church went to see *Raw!*"

"Not everyone, only two rows."

"Two rows!" she shouted as she tried to compose herself. "And where was the youth director?"

"About eight seats down," I sheepishly revealed.

Mom almost blew a gasket and was ready to beat some Christian ass when Dad decided to join the mêlée and help her out.

"Well, what did you think about the movie?" my dad sternly asked.

"It was bad, we didn't like it. I didn't like it."

He grinded harder.

"Are you trying to tell me you didn't like it?"

"No, we hated it. It wasn't funny at all." This was a bald-faced lie. I would have gut-punched Moses to meet Eddie Murphy.

"I've seen the movie," my dad exclaimed. "I know it's funny. Are you trying to tell me that you don't think Eddie Murphy is funny?"

At this point, my mom was rolling her eyes at my dad's superior parenting skills. She had no idea exactly where he was going with his questioning, nor did he; he was unsuccessfully adlibbing at this point.

"No, it wasn't funny at all," I lied.

"Eddie Murphy is hilarious; don't you lie to me."

I resisted.

"You didn't laugh once? Well, did you? Did you? Did you?" he raged.

I cracked.

"You're right, you're so right, I'm so sorry for lying. It was the funniest fucking shit I have ever seen in my life. It changed my life and I would leave you all today to be a funny black man," I bawled.

I did not actually say this. This was not a sitcom. Although derailing a train would not lead to an ass-beating, cussing at my parents would have. Removing the cuss words, it is indeed what I said.

The movie was funny as shit. To say differently would have been untruthful.

Oddly enough, this pissed my mom off more than anything we ever did. The *Raw* incident provided my mom with a welcome excuse to sever ties with Jesus. In doing so, she accomplished a couple things. Not only did she never have to suffer from our public humiliation, she would also avoid the preacher's poor pronunciation of our Lord's name, one of her biggest pet peeves. "Not even *Guh-haawwd* can save your heathen children."

This was the only time my mom gave in to parenting peer pressure. Afterwards, she realized that had she stuck to her guns and left us at the lake fishing, it would have saved her a lot of headaches. She also figured a well-deserving kid other than the Weathington Boys might need to win the yearly Easter Egg Hunt at some point.

In the end, we were dishonorably discharged from God's temple. I thought He would have had more endurance.

The Fire
(Our Coming out Party)
1984
10 years old

The summer between fourth and fifth grade was our most prolific, and we almost destroyed the entire town. Until then, we were infamous only in our own neighborhood. After the summer of 1984, the entire town would come to know the Weathington Boys. Looking back, I guess it isn't normal for ten-year-olds to have an armed stand off with the local fuzz, even if it was an inevitable trajectory.

Every kid — wait, every *normal* kid — plays with matches. Brian and I were no different except we might have taken our pyro antics a bit further than most. As I've mentioned, we also took our hobby to church, which might have pushed the limits of good taste. Over the years, we experimented with a variety of fire and explosive devices. Molotov cocktails were standard. They were cheap and easy, especially if you siphoned the gas, or unbolted the entire gas tank of a logging truck and took it home with you.

We referred to them as DD bombs, short for Daisy Duke bombs. Being huge fans of *The Dukes of Hazzard*, we loved the firebombs Bo and Luke used. At the time, though, it seemed a bit gay to name them Bo and Luke bombs. I guess the homophobia propaganda from church had had an impact on us.

We broke down fireworks and reassembled them into proper bombs. It was the country kid's version of the Manhattan Project. Using over the counter Snap n' Pops and some toilet paper we could make a firebomb that exploded on impact. Not many ten year olds can make a homemade mortar. So many match heads would make a nice torch. Hand grenades and landmines fashioned from shotgun shells were two of our better inventions.

How to make a hand grenade from a shotgun shell:
1. Cut plastic end off with pocketknife (the end where the lead comes out). If this is confusing, please stop reading immediately and continue shopping for your new sweater vest.
2. Shake out all lead.
3. Remove the wadding from the base of the brass. It is a small plastic vessel used to hold the lead. At point blank range it will leave a two-inch hole coming out.
4. Place a marble on the primer of the shotgun shell. This is the small inner circle on the brass end.
5. Tape the marble in place.
6. Throw.

The entire state of Georgia was withering from a protracted drought; not being farmers, we kids didn't pay it much attention. The year before, someone had logged all the trees from one of our local forests. As was par for the course in those days, nothing was replanted and a wasteland was left for everyone to enjoy for the next fifty or so years. There were piles of bone-dry pine trees as large as homes. What could possibly go wrong?

Brian and I, the only true thugs in the group, along with a couple of innocent bystanders were out on a walkabout. We lit a small fire on top of a hill. As it grew so did the entertainment value. The straight kids were panicky from the start, but I was really into it; I wanted it bigger.

I got my wish.

The fire quickly reached a level that was closing in on uncomfortable; we made the call to put it out. Everyone started stomping, beating it with the root balls of plants, and throwing large rocks: these techniques worked about as well as my mullet did on my first job interview. As we threw yet another rock on top of the pile, I noticed the fire fall into the hill. Like Han Solo realizing the *Millennium Falcon* was not parked in a cave, I realized we were not actually on a hill. Our hill was in fact the largest pile of dead pine trees in the Western Hemisphere. It was so large in comparison to the other 25-foot tall piles; we mistook it for a smallish mountain.

This was the turning point in our childhoods.

It got very big very fast. Brian ran by now in a full panic. I must have been a bit more of a pyro than Brian, because I was still kind of into it. Wait! Brian was in full panic! I was instantly slapped back into reality. If Brian was freaking out, I sure as hell should ramp up the adrenaline a notch. I then stepped back and took in the gravity of the situation. At this point, the fire was roughly the size of a small gymnasium and spreading like, well, wildfire, actually.

Brian sprinted for help. This was the second and last time either one of us: A) Left the scene of the crime without the other; B) Ran for help. Brian ran full tilt five miles to our house. My mom, forever posing as if she had normal children, had some of the local socialites over for lunch. They were probably discussing their honor roll sons and daughters and the next church fundraiser when Brian busted through the screened door.

Drenched in sweat and black ash, he collapsed at their feet. He was wearing his usual camouflaged cutoffs and no shirt. The sweat left white streaks through the ash on his skin like slug trails. My mom was shocked, but not nearly as much as her guests. She raised his head and asked him what was wrong. With his last available gasp he stated, "Fire."

My mom was temporarily struck with confusion until she looked in the direction from which he had run. Dark smoke was billowing skywards. No time for questions. Mom and a pack of neighbors converged on the fire with all the tools they could muster: hoes, shovels, buckets, and blankets, none of which did a damn thing.

When I first met the fire posse, I was running wind sprints between the fire and the creek with a one-gallon bucket. Like Brian, I was in a full sweat and covered in black ash. The only difference was that I was in cutoff blue jeans, not my camo shorts. We found twins that dressed the same to be odd.

Barely able to talk, I tried to tell my mom I didn't think her blankets would work. She was a strong, proud woman, and assured me that the blankets were the solution. Ordinarily, my mom could take care of everything. But there was nothing ordinary about this fire.

All the neighbors charged confidently up the hill. This confidence quickly eroded as they witnessed the second coming of the atomic bomb. No one could get within ten feet of the blaze, so hoes, shovels, and blankets were out. The buckets of water instantaneously transformed to steam before they hit the flames. The blankets, when they could get close enough, burnt like Underoos dipped in gasoline.

Now all the kids and adults were losing their shit, especially Brian who had now rejoined us. Seeing Mom and Brian panicking really pushed me over the edge. They were both shoveling dirt with an inefficient spasmodic motion. My vision blurred with tears as I thought about all our friends who would die in the fire that we started to entertain ourselves. Was the world about to end at the hands of the Weathington Boys? Everyone retreated. Mom called the fire department.

We were sent to our room in hopes of calming us down. This is exactly what did not happen.

As I've mentioned, Bremen is a very small town. The fire department and the police station were in the same building and staffed by the same people. Unsure of exactly what type of catastrophe they were being called to, they split up and brought both the fire trucks and the police cars. Tension was escalating much like the fire roaring in the distance. Like most small towns, we also had a collection of ambulance, fire truck, and police car chasers. Anytime they were dispatched, the same parade of people followed. This procession then attracted any and all nosy neighbors, who then had to call their friends who called their friends to come see what in the Sam Hill was going on in Mountain Shadows.

Every time we glanced out the window, the crowd was bigger. As it grew, so did the level of anxiety in the room. When the crowd was roughly over 200 people, something unique happened. I hate to admit it, but the Weathington Boys officially went into freak-out mode. This is not the same as rage, anxiety, panic, or fear. It is where all rational thought takes off like O.J. after he found his wife and her boyfriend had fallen and impaled themselves on his butcher knife 43 times. Not including the time Brian spent the night in a dumpster in college, this was the one and only time either of us completely lost our shit.

The firemen took all their trucks and equipment to the fire. They were outmatched. Their only hope was to dig a trench around it and hope it would burn itself out.

The fire was all but forgotten in our minds; we had moved on to our imminent jail time and we were not going in without a fight. As far as Brian and I were concerned, the police were not going to take us alive. We built a barricade by cleverly arranging our bunk beds directly against the back wall extending straight into the door. Brian and I got out the pellet guns.

"What about the 10-pump rule!?!"

"Screw the 10-pump rule!"

Once our guns were fully pumped and we were in position I noticed one of the straight kids was trembling in the corner of our bedroom. When he uncovered his face I realized it was the kid from Syria. Solid kid, but he would need years of training to be ready for this level of shit show, training he most likely would have received in his homeland.

"What's going on?" Syria said with a shaky voice.

"They're gonna bust in here and take us to jail!" Brian yelled, froth in the corner of his mouth.

Syria was given a bat; he hadn't been awarded his pellet gun merit badge yet.

The police chief knocked on our door and told us he was coming in. He should have asked. It did not take him long to realize this was not going to be a routine traffic stop. Irritated, he told us he was going to bust in the door. This was gasoline on the fire. Pun intended. It was kind of like the last scene in *Young Guns* where Charlie nuts out, but instead of Charlie, picture two Ultimate Warriors on meth and you have the scene in our bedroom.

The guns were out, and we were shooting to kill. You would have to be lucky to kill someone with a pellet gun, but God knows we had them pumped up enough. Syria was now in the fetal position in a corner. To his credit, he had not released the bat. However, he was dead to us; we knew he wouldn't be a factor in this battle.

Brian and I continued to pepper the door with pellets every time the cops shoved the door hard enough to open a crack. We were really coming into our own. Maybe they were snickering on the other side of the door, but in our minds their guns were drawn and they were coming in for the kill. We were not backing down.

The standoff continued for several hours as they would regroup and try other strategies. They talked to us, tricked us, and even attempted a sneak attack to ram open the door. Doors are always busted open on TV with little effort. Not this door. Not this time.

Our next move was to survey out the window. Our room was up about fifteen feet from the ground, a fall that would hurt even the most durable of kids. A tree was about an eight-foot leap from the windowsill. We had the window open and were preparing our Jimmy Superfly Snuka escape, when reason knocked on the door.

Eventually they sent in their only hope: Mom. She

calmly told the officers if they wanted her to talk us down, they would need to be out of sight and silent. After 20 minutes of talking, we agreed to remove the barricade and come out. I would like to believe that my mom was not a part of the next scene.

Bremen's finest sprang out of hiding in full SWAT formation. They grabbed us and dragged us to the dining room table in cuffs. Syria was left hiding under the bed. I guess, given the fact that we had been shooting at them, this was indeed necessary and appropriate force.

At the dining room table in cuffs and cutoffs, the cops read us our rights. Brian and I both tried to wipe away the tears leaving us looking like bizarre white-eyed raccoons. This was the only time I would ever see Brian cry. We had officially lost our criminal virginity.

Eventually the crowd dissipated and the fire was safely sealed off, if not totally under control. It was still smoldering two months later. As part of our probation, the firemen and cops left us with some harsh documentation outlining what we could and could not do for the next three years of our lives.

When it was all said and done, my family took their places at the dinner table. This would have been a very appropriate time for them to beat and berate the shit out of us. However, they did not. My parents knew we were shaken up and were truly scared for the first time in our lives; add to that the exhaustion of fire fighting, sprinting, freaking-out, and the armed standoff. They trusted we had learned our lesson and were on a path to being normal members of society.

They should have beat the shit out of us.

If the Train should Jump the Tracks

1984

10 years old

Had they beat that ass, this book would have been shorter; instead the heat was back on us four weeks later. The sting of our first arrest wore off a bit faster than one might guess.

Although some old-school corporal punishment might have prevented future felonies, in my opinion, it would have been a short-lived victory. You can't beat out industrious ingenuity; it only gets buried to resurface as another bad habit, potentially worse than the first. We were mini MacGyvers, and unlike our Swiss-Knife-carrying friend, we had no moral hang-ups when it came to firearms. Had our parents forced us inside we would have just brought this behavior to the basement and potentially started a meth lab. Freedom was a better long-term strategy.

As official outlaws, we needed a hideout. Not far from our house was quite possibly the coolest hideout any young ruffian could ask for. Brian, Ashley, and I, along with four other members of our crew, took up residence in a set of boxcars that were stored off to the side of the main tracks. They were homely at first, but we spruced the place up with couches, a swing set, secret compartments, and a touch of spray paint. Interior decorating only kept us entertained for so long.

The three of us quickly figured out the schedules of all the trains and could interpret the different light signals in the control box. Since we knew when they were coming, an ambush was unavoidable. At first, it was innocent activities such as flattening pennies. There is no need to call *MythBusters*; a penny will not derail a train. This is an urban legend for kids who didn't have sex in high school and whose parents wear golf shirts while drinking white zinfandel on the veranda. In fact, quarters, nuts, bolts, rocks, and trees will not derail a train, although I don't recommend trying it.

After testing everything known to man, we mounted a full-scale attack four times a day on passing trains, pelting them with rocks, spare railroad spikes, and buckets of paint. I love the edgy rebellious kids nowadays who are daring enough to spray paint their initials on the backside of an abandoned building. These are the same kids who will later complain at the clubhouse about their exhaustion from driving a miniature car two miles while drinking a six-pack of Bud Heavy and swinging a club at a small white stationary ball with dimples. Their dad was probably killed in a slap fight. Try throwing a gallon of purple paint at a white train car going 50 mph. It is daring, unique, and artistic. It was Jackson Pollock but faster, cheaper, and on tour across the country 24/7.

Although I excelled in physics, what happened next defies logic. The four o'clock was being ambushed from the convenience of our hideout. Brian looked over to signal the caboose was coming. The caboose, the sweet spot of the ambush, occasionally blessed us with an operator to harass. Between us sat a five-gallon bucket of rocks, compliments of the train companies themselves. Granite chunks littered the tracks, and they were practically begging for it if you ask me.

As the car approached, I chunked my rock at the front to try to squeeze it between the last car and the caboose. I hit my target, but only the steel. The caboose made a better noise when you hit it, or least we thought it did. Brian waited until the caboose was directly broad side to release the hounds.

This magical piece of granite did not actually strike the caboose. It skimmed directly parallel to the back wall of the caboose. Given the wall was moving from right to left at 50 mph and the rock was thrown directly forward, it should have been impossible for the rock to fly parallel to the back wall. But it wasn't.

This little anomaly of physics made the Kennedy lone gunman theory seem more plausible. The only explanation I can come up with is the mystical rock was caught in the back draft made by the wind and pulled forward in what amounted to the sickest curveball ever thrown. Unbeknownst to us, the caboose operator was getting some shuteye as the train whizzed across the country. He was propped against the back wall in a wooden chair. His alarm clock was about to go off.

As I have mentioned before, Brian had a cannon for an arm. This rock was realistically doing 55 mph, and with the train moving in a different direction at 50 mph it carried significant force. The conductor took it straight in the jaw. He fell like Nancy Kerrigan if Bo Jackson was swinging the bat instead of Tonya's white trash ex-husband. Thank God he didn't fall off the train and get killed; this story wouldn't be nearly as funny.

Several seconds passed while he shook it off and put together what the hell had happened. The caboose was now a hundred feet away and moving rapidly. He struggled to his feet, grabbed the rock, and while shaking it at Brian, yelled out a phrase that is as vivid in my mind today as when I was ten years old.

"I'm gonna make you eat this!"

As the train disappeared into the sunset, silence filled the hideout. We had just witnessed something special and we needed to mark it with the appropriate amount of respect. This was quite possibly the greatest throw in the history of delinquency. It would only be rivaled by Ashley's Money Shot the following year. Everyone congratulated Brian as if he had just pitched a perfect game in the World Series. I was so proud of him, yet jealous that I had not thrown the kill shot.

Being industrious, ingenious little bastards and quick to fill the void left by the Great Throw, we turned to learning everything there was to know about the mechanics of a train car, assisted by Ashley's realistic train set at home. We learned how to separate the cars and release a variety of brakes to set the cars in motion.

The result: Thousands of tons of steel on the move with ten-year-olds at the helm. We rolled the train cars down the tracks and assembled them in a variety of configurations. There was always someone ready to hit the brakes to keep them from going all the way down the hill. Yes, we were riding them. Later this would become a major form of transportation for us.

After watching them stop and go in the hoodlum version of Red-Light, Green-Light, we decided to see what would happen if we let them continue down the hill. Luckily, the smart train people had built a contraption called a derailer to prevent these cars from going onto the main tracks and causing a real train disaster. We weren't aware of this contraption.

Our set of 20 train cars, including our three huts, began to pick up speed. We ran alongside the cars to see if we could keep up. Suddenly, hell rained down on us. It is impossible to fully appreciate the noise a derailed train makes unless you've been there. I have been there, and let me tell you, it was emotional.

Everyone quickly realized what was going on. Cars began to topple. Most of us leaped at full speed off the steep cliff into a large mass of conveniently placed kudzu. It is moments like this when I believe in God. This kudzu was like jumping into a pile of feather pillows.

We did a quick headcount and realized that besides a few scratches, everyone was okay. We hid in a thicket of trees a few hundred yards away to consider the incident. Although Ashley was the third voting member of the gang, Brian and I were the only ones with a RAP sheet, and everyone looked to us for advice.

After the fire, Brian and I sat up many nights after the "incident" and discussed what we could have done different. It never crossed our minds to not do it in the first place. We covered strategies, escapes, and communication with adults. During this debriefing session, we produced the survival plan for the rest of our childhood. One might call it our mission statement. It consisted of three points.

First: Always be one step ahead of all adults. Normal adults cannot think like young thugs no matter how hard they try.

Second: Run, run, and run some more. Do not look back and do not get caught. We were *Chariots of Fire* minus the shitty piano music.

Third: If caught, lie, lie, and lie some more. Never admit anything, never rat on a friend, and never back down.

We now shared this mission statement with the group. Its merits were agreed upon and everyone bought in. Sworn to secrecy, the gang left the scene and agreed not to meet for a few weeks until things cooled down. As we were leaving, Brian and I looked back at the carnage. Over half the cars were on their side with the others bent over in lewd positions.

"That was a cool hut, wasn't it," Brian said.

"Yeah."

Brian and I barely spoke to each other about the incident for fear of being overheard. Everyone kept his oath.

Several weeks passed and we had all but forgotten the derailment. Brian and I were throwing a football in the front yard when a plain car — the kind of plain that draws attention to itself — approached our driveway. The driver rolled down his window and asked where one of our friends lived. After I obliged, he asked if I knew where Nathan Weathington lived. I quickly answered, "Hey, that's me!" I thought I had won something. What a dumb-ass.

The undercover Smokey quickly slid his car sideways to block our escape. It was a nice and necessary maneuver. He now knew where we lived, so we were instantly to the third bullet point of our mission statement. Outwitting and outrunning were already off the table. The man was stern, and his physique told us he would not be easily distracted by fresh donuts like our rounder local fuzz. Our first experience with the feds.

Our parents were not home. The man led us inside to our dining room, his de facto interrogation room. Once again, we had our rights read at the dining room table while in cuffs and cutoffs. Talk about déjà vu.

Then the rapid-fire questions started. Had we ever been to the train tracks? No. Had we ever thrown rocks at trains? No. Had we ever placed things on the railroad tracks? No. Had we ever derailed a train? No. Deny, deny, deny. We were holding our own against this criminal mastermind.

"Are you sure you know nothing about any train cars up at the dirt field?" the Smokey asked.

"Yessir," we both remarked.

This is when he opened his briefcase and things went off the rails <Insert comedy drummer here>. He placed a set of photos on the table showing the gang in a variety of compromising positions. Those bastards had hidden on top of the oil tankers 100 yards away up 75 feet in the air and photographed us with what must have been one hell of a telephoto lens.

The pictures showed Brian, Ashley, and me putting stuff on the tracks, pelting the train cars with rocks, and operating the brakes on the cars. Regrettably, they did not have a photo of Brian's miraculous caboose shot. Come to think of it, that is probably when the surveillance started. Our deny, deny, deny strategy was getting harder, harder, harder.

Smokey then told us he knew about our earlier conviction and figured this incident might send us to Y.D.C. If you were a typical child, you would not know what Y.D.C. stands for. It stands for Youth Detention Center, a.k.a. Juvie. This put a lump in my throat. I was not ready for group showers.

Brian and I were losing hope when Dad walked through the door. I did not even hear him drive up. He looked over at us in complete confusion, rightfully so.

When the man turned to face him, Dad asked, "Jonathan, what are you doing here?"

Being the head football coach, and man about town in general, meant my dad knew everyone within a fifty-mile radius. In addition, if you were interested in football or had ever played football, his network increased to include several surrounding states.

"Larry?"

"What's going on, Jonathan?"

"Are these your sons?"

"I'm afraid so. What'd they do?"

"It's pretty serious."

Turns out my dad and "Jonathan" were football chums from high school. My dad grabbed them both a beer and they went to the back deck. They left us at the dining room table alone. This is a tactic called "sweating them out" that we have been the victims of many times since.

In fact, fifteen years later, a company employed this technique on Brian during an interview for a sales position. He quickly recognized this method and got up and left.

As he was walking out, the interviewer ran after him and frantically asked where he was going. Brian informed him he did not have time for their childish bullshit and to quit screwing around with him. They did not even bother with the rest of the candidates and hired him on the spot. He is now the top rep in their company.

After an hour or so, they both returned. Jonathan said his goodbyes, uncuffed us and left out the front door. We had indeed been officially arrested. We had, however, avoided gang rape, which is always a good thing. The saving of our buttholes was due to the simple fact that my dad was the lead blocker for Jonathan who played tailback in high school. God bless football. We were now on not-so-top-secret double probation.

During football season my dad barely had time to breathe. I can only guess he did not have the energy to beat us or even to properly yell at us. He looked exhausted and went to bed as soon as my mom made it home.

"Really? It hasn't been a month," she said.

"We're really sorry. It was an accident."

"What should I do with you two?"

"I don't know," I said with my head hung. It killed both of us to see Mom upset.

"Go to your room. We can talk about this tomorrow morning. I need a glass of wine right now."

The next day our parents compared notes with Ashley's parents. Although we all now had police records, Brian's and my second of the summer, there were more pressing issues at hand. Jonathan let us off light, but the train company still wanted us to pay to get the cars back on the tracks. Our parents could not afford to put even a toy train back on its tracks and they were worried.

Luckily, Ashley's mom was a social worker and had been around other juvenile delinquents in a courtroom. She explained to the train official that the boxcar was an "attractive nuisance", which I think meant it was the most badass ten-year-old hideout on the planet. Apparently, this was the magic phrase.

There were still a variety of stipulations to our probation which overlapped the requirements of the first probation. We were not allowed within 100 feet of railroad tracks until we were 18 years old unless our parents were driving us over them. This is difficult in a town surrounded on all sides by train tracks.

After the train incident, we went underground like the A-Team, and our mug shots never surfaced again until high school.

But if you egg the principal's wife at point blank range you should expect something to go down.

Little Red Corvette
1984
10 years old

People say good things come in threes; my mom is not one of those people. The summer of 1984 took its toll on my mom, and she began to question her parenting style — we were arrested three times in two and half months. We were seriously getting on it. My mom and dad could have used a little more Orwellian mind control in their 1984.

A car dealership was going up at the edge of our neighborhood, providing us all kinds of new games to play. Hiding in dirt piles, we lobbed dirt clod hand grenades at the construction workers. After they left, we would pilfer the site for anything worth stealing, destroying, or dropping from extreme heights. A case of hot Cokes was the most interesting thing we found until we discovered the Magic Tape.

The Magic Tape looked like a thick web of masking tape, but along with the normal sticky side it had a white tacky gum substance down the middle. We had never seen tape like this, and I have not seen it since. This stuff was badass; it would pull the green off Lou Ferrigno.

The whole gang was on thin ice for the rest of the summer, and even Brian and I were treading lightly, given our two prior convictions. I continue to maintain we were not looking for trouble on this particular day, but it just happened to ride up with the top off.

While continuing with our dirt clod battle we discussed all the applications of our new found Magic Tape. Someone suggested it was strong enough to dangle one of us off the roof; others figured it could be used to catch wild animals. The idea that intrigued us the most was using it as a roadside bomb. Someone suggested we could stretch the tape across the road and stick bundles of bottles on each end, and when a car ran over the tape, the bottles would crash into its sides. We all agreed that, although it would be neat, there was no way it would actually work.

If only to prove the futility of the plan, Brian and I stretched the tape across the road as the others stuck bottles on the ends.

"It looks good. But a car would be going too fast for it to stick," Brian commented.

"Let's pull it up," I answered.

But before we had time to think, a brand new shiny red t-top Corvette pulled into the neighborhood. We stood paralyzed like a dumbass opossum on the road, assuming the car would drive over it and nothing would happen. No one bothered to hide.

The man driving was wearing a wife-beater tank top, sporting a pimp-stache, and accessorized with a gold chain. He leaned out the window and saw the tape on the road, and for some reason thought this was the chance to prove his manhood to his bikini-clad copilot.

The front tires went over it without incident. The back tires — not so much. As he approached the roadside bomb the driver goosed it, balling the tires over the magic tape. Maybe it was the weight in the back, maybe it was the extra torque or width of the hotrod tires, but whatever the reason, the back tires did indeed stick to the tape.

With the tires spinning rapidly, the bottles quickly spooled into the side of the car's shiny candy shell. Both sets of bottles hit the car like a piñata. Glass flew off the sides in every direction and even landed around our feet. The man slammed on the brakes and jumped from the car. He took one look at his pride and joy and went into one of the finest cussing tirades the world has ever heard. We were adding a new word every sentence or two to our already solid vocabulary, courtesy of the honorable Eddie Murphy. His sexy copilot tried to come to our rescue, jumping from her seat in an effort to calm him down. When she reached our side and saw the damage, she stopped in her tracks. "Holy shit!" she yelled, and then she started cussing at us as well. Barbie was not as skilled a linguist as the driver, but she made up for it in her racially charged, yet highly seductive, rebel flag two-piece.

The man said he was going to the cops. I knew this meant juvie. A third arrest during one summer break would surely land us behind bars. I hid my tears as he stormed to his car. He was about to get in when he steamed back over to us.

"What's yer name, son?" he shouted at Brian.

In what will go down as the coolest, most intelligent thing ever uttered by a ten-year-old, Brian looked at the man and calmly said, "Wes Smithermen." Oh how quickly the tables had turned; Brian now had the upper hand. A false name — I should have thought of that. This is not the type of thing a ten-year-old could pull off now. Today's sweet nuggets are hovered over on playgrounds as if they were carrying plutonium, leading to an inability to think their way out of a paper bag. It did not take me long to catch on; I used my tears to my advantage.

"Matt Smithermen," I said solemnly. I almost screwed this up and said a different last name until I remembered we looked exactly freakin' alike. Brian would have hit me with his bat had I screwed up his line. He recognized Brian and me as the ringleaders and did not bother questioning the minions. Good thing too; they would have cracked for sure.

The man peeled out of there and went straight to the cops. Brian and I took off like shoppers at K-Mart with a blue light special on free smokes. We pedaled our Spiderman bikes faster than their recommended top speed: we needed to get home and off the road before the cops arrived. We were scared shitless and decided to brief my mom on the incident. Once again she came to our rescue.

Calming us down with graham crackers and peanut butter, she then joined us to peer out the window, expecting the Bremen P.D. to show up at anytime. We waited and waited; nothing happened. Our mom was quite relieved. She didn't want to deal with the fuzz any more than we did, and she didn't want her babies violated in jail either — such love. This was the First Commandment in the Book of Marilyn; Mom figured if she loved us and we knew we were loved that everything else would take care of itself. In my opinion, it worked. Others might disagree.

No one slept well that night. Our dad got home late, and Mom decided not to tell him about our little confrontation. It was for the best. The next morning we all went to school in Godzilla, a luxury green, fake wood paneled station wagon customized with permanently affixed *Dukes of Hazzard* stickers on all smooth surfaces.

"You boys should look over at the cool car at Richie's," she said.

Richie's was a service station where Brian and I would later work our first summer jobs. Up on the racks was a lovely red Corvette having two new back tires installed. Mom was sly. Dad never looked up from the football play on his yellow legal pad. We understood then why the police never came. The man had to walk the last mile to the police station after his tires blew out, or maybe he didn't make it at all, or maybe the SWAT team was out busting the Smithermen brothers' ass. Either way, they never cuffed us, and we knew we had the coolest mom on the planet.

The Money Shot
1985
11 years old

In my life, I have experienced six truly pure things: Brian's rock throw, sight fishing for trout, my boys' laugh when they realize that I am actually changing their diaper, Hemingway's *Old Man and the Sea*, my mom's banana bread, and Ashley Sanders's sick-ass egg throw of 1985. Everyone will remember where they were when they heard about 9/11 and the shuttle explosion. I can tell you not only where I was, but also what I was wearing and what flavor of gum I was chewing when the sky parted and I witnessed a miracle in 1985. (It was Hubba Bubba watermelon, if you were wondering.)

It isn't fair to compare Ashley's Money Shot to Brian's rock throw at the train. Both were equally pure and beautiful, and it is my book, so I am not picking a favorite.

Brian, Ashley, and I had been invited to one of the straight kids' birthday party; let's call him Russell. There were around twenty kids attending. The group had heard stories about us and wanted us to spice up their party a bit. We obliged.

Today's birthday parties are more exciting than Disney World. The last one I went to literally had Barney waddling around. How do you even go about booking that fat purple freak? What am I to do now, go out and book Santa Claus for my son's birthday party in July? Thanks, assholes. These dipshits also gave their daughter twenty dollars for losing her first tooth, causing a trickle-down effect amongst the entire elementary school.

We rode to the party in the back of my dad's black GMC pickup. My dad called us over to his window as we prepared to make a run on the giant bowl of Ho-Hos in the front yard.

My sons now eat food that I don't even recognize. Quinoa? I thought that was a country in the South Pacific. What the hell are shade-grown, fair trade, free range organic eggs? Does that even come out of a chicken? Their hot dogs are actually good for them. It's a hot dog — it's supposed to be lips and asses; that's the point. They eat cereal with no prizes in the box and with enough fiber to keep all of Del Boca Vista regular.

"Don't do anything stupid please," my dad said.

After the usual cookout and cake, the troop took off on a walk through the woods. When we came to the road, the host of the party pulled out two dozen eggs. He summoned all his courage and stated we were to egg the next car that came by. This made 17 of the kids excitedly nervous. Three were not; this was not our first rodeo.

The mob was pumped. Everyone received one egg and then we waited, and waited, and waited. The straight kids seemed very relieved by the lack of cars, whereas Brian, Ashley, and I were a bit pissed at the lack of action. Collectively we must have played a thousand games of Slaps during the intermission. The birthday boy must have picked the slowest road in the county. After about 45 minutes, we finally saw headlights.

As the car got closer, the tension in the group escalated. The nervous energy in the air reached unbearable levels and the crowd crept further and further back from the road. Like a herd of antelope, once one of them bolted, they all started running. We were baffled by their behavior. I'm not sure what the hell they were running from; they hadn't done anything and their eggs were all busted on the ground.

And then there were three ...

I looked over at Brian and Ashley and calmly said, "Why the hell not?"

"Well, we aren't baking a cake with these eggs," Brian joked.

"Get ready, it's almost here," Ashley chimed in.

At this point, the Earth stopped spinning, or at least slowed down significantly. The next 28 seconds stretched into as many days. It was the most surreal and incredible moment of my life. I should say my wedding or the birth of my children holds this honor, but I would be lying.

The black Pontiac Trans Am, complete with gold bird on the hood, approached at full speed. The car was on the opposite side of the street. I threw first and my egg flew over the windshield without being noticed. Brian once again delivered — he hit the front left quarter-panel. This got the driver's attention.

While slamming on the brakes, the man jerked his head back to see where the egg had come from. Ashley had let his fly directly behind Brian's. As the man looked back, I realized his face was slightly out of the half-open window. Ashley's amazing egg was heading straight for our victim's face. The force of the car coming to a stop in one direction, coupled with the force of Ashley's egg going in the opposite direction made for an excellent Algebra II word problem.

The egg appeared to stall in midair like an odd-shaped nocturnal hummingbird. By some act of God, the magic egg found its way through the six-inch gap in the window and struck the Bandit right between the eyes. Now, I do not mean the cliché "I hit him right between the eyes." I mean it literally struck him on the bridge of his nose, which was slap-dab between his beady eyes. His head popped back like Sly's in the first *Rocky* (before Mickey actually taught him any defense — what a lousy manager).

Just like Brian's throw, there was an accompanying moment of silence. None of us could believe it. We were paralyzed, our mouths agape in disbelief, as if we had just learned Darth Vader was Luke's father for the first time. My gum fell from my mouth. Ashley snickered, breaking the spell. We started to laugh.

"I'm gonna *kill* you little shits!" the man yelled.

"I think that's our cue," I said.

We took off through the forest. He could not keep up. We ran in the opposite direction of the house we had come from. That was common sense, or at least we thought so.

The other kids were jogging like a flock of dodo birds back to the birthday boy's house. Mr. Bandit easily spotted them and followed them back. The three of us watched from the bushes as he knocked on the door. The parents opened the door and after a brief explanation appeared appropriately horrified by the man's story.

All the kids were reprimanded and directed to clean the man's car. The entire pack went to town on that car. When they were done, Stroker Ace could have eaten his Chicken Pit sandwich off that bird.

We waited in the bushes until they were putting the finishing touches on the Trans Am. As we strolled up, Brian asked the group what was going on. They explained they had been busted egging the man's car. Thankfully, it was too dark for the Bandit to identify us.

Brian feigned confusion. "Someone egged a car?"

The darkness combined with the anonymity of the pack had provided us with the perfect cover. We were home free and didn't even have to clean the car. Now three decades later, the other 17 kids will finally learn who actually threw that magic egg.

Mr. Bandit then exited the house with a towel in hand. I looked up and saw egg still stuck in the cracks of his eyes, his Bandit mustache, and his heinous permed skullet, a cross between David Hasselhoff and a balding Sissy Spacek. I almost shit my pants I was straining so hard not to laugh. We all three were forced back to the bushes to compose ourselves.

As far as our parents were concerned we had finally behaved ourselves, and we were rewarded with a trip to the Bass Pro Shop.

The straight kids wanted a party, and although they didn't know it, we gave them one.

We were Running
1988
14 years old

Ray Womack out-badassed the Weathington Boys. When we met Ray in the third grade he already carried a knife and could drive a stick better than most amateur racecar drivers. On one of our first "play dates" Ray hotwired the neighbor's baby blue Chevette and drove us to the local pool hall where we picked the locks on the tables and used all the quarters to gamble on a punch board bingo game. My wife continues to call bullshit on this Ray driving factoid, but no one from Bremen does.

To help his family make ends meet, Ray worked with his dad breaking down and reassembling diesel engines. Like his dad, Ray would also become a skilled carpenter, plumber, welder, and electrician. Ray routinely became a foreman within the first week of showing up on any job site. To sum it up, imagine B.A. Baracus as a young white boy with more talent, less gold, and 150 pounds less muscle, and you have Ray Womack.

Ray also had several oddball talents, one of which was arm wrestling. Despite being a string bean when we first met him, Ray could easily beat Brian, me, and any other kid who wanted to make a small wager on the strength of his arm. He has always attributed this talent to his superior lug nut strength.

One of his other talents was that he was a nasty rope swing cowboy. His signature move was a double back-flip preacher-seat combo — an impressive dive on its own, but made more so by the fact that Ray could not swim worth a damn. When I recently asked him about this peculiarity, he said he figured since Brian and I could swim, we would save him if he was unable to doggy paddle to safety. This talent also earned him the nickname "Corndog Ray" after a character of the same name appeared on a rope swing in a Jeff Foxworthy book. Ray won a bull riding competition once, despite the fact that he had never even ridden a horse. If Brian was De Niro in cutoffs, and I was Geordie in *Stand by Me*, Ray was a cross between Burt Reynolds and Kid Rock.

Brian and I have been tied to the hip with Ray since the third grade, so it's odd that I'm this far into the book before needing to introduce him. But our early years with Ray didn't really fit the format of these stories. When we were hanging out with Ray we went 100 percent feral. Our debauchery always took place ten miles back in the woods, so we didn't have many run-ins with the cops, or anyone else for that matter, and thus no strong punch line. It was one of those "if a tree falls in the woods" situations. Let's just say many did and no one heard. While at Ray's house we usually shot at least 500 rounds of ammo a weekend, and by the time we reached high school we would have held our own against a platoon of snipers.

We ran from everyone. Sprinting through the woods with someone in hot pursuit was a thrill, and the closer we could lure them in the better. We were fit, knew our way through the blackest woods, and were willing to run through briars, swamps, or bush if need be. So if we didn't beat them with our fitness, we would fall back on our stupidity and high tolerance for pain and grime. A list of all our track and field escapades is beyond the scope of this book, but I will tell you about one that kind of sums it up.

We exhausted our parents during the day, so they slept soundly at night, leaving them vulnerable and oblivious. Once my parents were asleep, we would sneak out the basement door and begin our adventures. On the lam, we would hike for hours through town and through the woods to get to our ambush locations, which could be as far as ten miles away. For some reason, we never had flashlights and would always end up with bruised shins and scrapes on our faces from running into things in the middle of the night.

On one notorious occasion, Brian, Ashley, Ray, and I were all out on the same mission. Four vote-casting members of the gang in the same place would inevitably lead to trouble. There were also several straight kids, but they were all solid second-stringers on the hooligan depth chart and need no further description. Once we reached Piggly Wiggly we started scheming.

It didn't take long to rearrange the letters on the signs to spell all the vulgarities we knew at the time. In what would become one of our classic moves, one of us would run a grocery cart to the top of the flagpole while someone else climbed up to cut off the ropes and tie them to the top of the pole. They would be flying the gangly cart flag for weeks if not months. And we always threw in some random vandalism to keep things spicy. All of these things were fun, but not very creative.

We found a large mountain of used tires next to a service station, perfect for a civilized game of king of the mountain. Whoever made it to the top first would throw tires down at the kids trying to dethrone him. We had to be fast to not get smacked in the late night reality version of *Donkey Kong*. This entertained us for a while, but then a light bulb came on — we decided the cars on the highway ought to be Mario.

Everyone grabbed tires from the service station and went to the top of the hill. We each ran several trips to build three large stacks of tires, one on each side of the street and one in the middle. It was a slow highway. The plan: wait until a car was halfway down the adjacent hill before releasing the Michelin man on its ass.

"I see lights!" Ray yelled.

"Easy tiger, we need to wait," I told the group. We didn't want to jump the gun and have our tires fall flaccid on the road before the car reached them.

We waited as long as we could. "Now!" I screamed. Everyone started rolling tires down the hill: tractor tires, Yugo tires, truck tires, an eclectic mix of rubber and steel. Each one of us set in motion around ten tires. With the help of a full moon I could see around 70 tires silently speeding downhill. The road was four lanes wide, which minimized the gutter balls.

The law of convergence can be a wonderful thing. The first surge of tires met the car at exactly the trough of the two hills, at the point where the tires were at maximum velocity. It was a large hill; the tires were smoking along and bouncing several feet off the ground every time they hit a bump in the road. Mario was in deep shit.

The burgundy IROC was caught off guard. He swerved around the first semi-tire only to run head first into a 205 70R15 which rolled straight over the hood like BIGFOOT. The car began swerving side to side, screeching its tires to avoid the inevitable onslaught.

We watched the show from our pre-arranged hideout, ironically, behind the mountain of tires. I had to bite my arm to keep from laughing out loud. The driver stopped and got out of the car in hopes of avoiding more damage. His car continued to be pummeled with ten or more tires as our reinforcements reached the front lines. Even if he saw them coming, they were coming too hard for him to fend them off by hand. The silence between collisions was somewhat sexual and my extremities began to tingle.

The man was completely baffled; he had no idea where to even start looking for the guilty parties who had destroyed his car. He finally gave up and continued on his way as we regrouped and prepared for the next battle. We continued with the ambush for two more rounds on a Red Fiero, not to be confused with a Ferrari, and a primer-grey Nova. Our goal was to whip up some pig action. The swine heard our mating call.

Two Smokies topped the hill with lights flashing; unfortunately, we only had a handful of tires at the time. We shoved ten down and hoped for the best. From the comfort of our hideout, we watched some fancy maneuvering from Bremen's finest. The lead car must have been driven by a country boy; he showed mad skills. I'm sorry to say his wingman did not. It was as if Wingman was trying to hit them. Hell, we only rolled ten tires and they were spread out over four lanes, and somehow *Driving Miss Daisy* managed to hit at least seven of them. None of us even had a learner's permit and we would have faired far better than this idiot.

Once the brief mêlée subsided, the cops got out of their cars and searched for the perps using their high-powered spotlights. They were hopeless. They were about two years away from catching us when Brian decided to throw them a bone.

"You boys ready?" Brian asked, signaling to the world he was about to do something which would require you to run for your life. This was one of Brian Weathington's famous rhetorical questions. No one ever bothered to answer. Everyone got ready to run.

Brian and I worked at a service station at the time and were milliseconds away from making a NASCAR pit crew. We'd also learned some clever tricks for moving tires across a parking lot with minimum effort.

When the cops weren't looking, Brian went to the front of tire mountain and placed a large tire face down and kicked up at 45 degrees. With a 165 85R 20 all-weather number in hand he climbed to the top of Tire Mountain. The pile of tires was located uphill from where the cops had parked their cars and were now socializing about how inept they were at their jobs. Brian perched on top of the hill like *King Kong*, lifted the tire vertically and slammed it down onto the angled tire — instant acceleration. Brian had launched a tire torpedo at the cops.

The two dodged the tire as it took the head Smokie's side mirror off. They came sprinting at us, which would really be better described as a light jog, although they were working hard and should be commended for their effort. As the cops approached, the second-string kids took off. They were all skilled sprinters, the slow ones having been eaten years before.

None of our parents obsessively pushed us to become the next Williams' sisters. We were pretty damn good athletes despite not having a personal trainer in middle school. I don't want to give the impression that I'm immune or somehow superior to this type of nonsense. It's easy to get caught up in the madness. In an effort to make sure my son is physically superior to his kickball playmates, we both ended up in yoga together, him at two-and-a-half and me as the guy who looked like he could eat the yogi. There must be too much patchouli in the water here on the West Coast. As I bent down in a comprising squat thrust, malasana to you self-righteously flexible folks, my son looked up, confused.

"Dada. Do you have to poo?"

"No. Do you wanna get out of here?"

"Yes, Dada."

"How about a milkshake?"

"Yes, Dada!"

"We're gone," I said to the stickman at the front of the class. He might have been flexible, but my oldest son was about ten pounds of muscle away from being able to beat his ass.

Back at Tire Mountain, only the four vets were left, the smokies were approaching, and the game of Chicken had started. No one said we were playing Chicken, no one explained the rules, but everyone knew the game and all four of us were in. Whoever ran from the cops last was the top dog. Pretty self-explanatory. The clock was ticking.

They approached with flashlights out and hands on their guns. Thirty feet out, no one moved — we just stared and grinned at each other. Twenty feet out, everyone was still ice cold. Fifteen feet out, Ashley took off. Ten feet out, I bolted. I looked back as the cops moved, now inches away from Brian and Ray.

I am thoroughly convinced that Brian and Ray, if left alone for any length of time, would cause a disaster of mythic proportions. As I glanced behind me, Brian and Ray had their heads on a swivel glancing at the cops and then at each other waiting for the first flinch. The cops were within arms' reach of Tweedle Dee and Tweedle Dumb when they both bolted at roughly the same time. The race was on.

I am not sure why they bothered to chase us. No bookie would have taken bets on them at any odds. The two of them were easily pushing three bucks apiece. They also had on their *Batman* tool belts that looked to weigh 15 pounds. In combination with those polyester button-up clothes and army boots, Carl Lewis they were not.

It was too dark for them to be able to identify us, and we had to continually slow down to stay within their sight. Brian, Ray, Ashley, and I were now talking casually as we jogged. After less than a half-mile, the boys in blue gave up and opted for yelling at us to come back, but they were so winded we could barely hear them.

We continued with our run and made it back to my house in time to grab an obnoxiously large waffle breakfast. "If you feed them, they will come," was another tenet central to Mom's parenting philosophy. This kept us coming back every meal to allow her to check us for scars, snakebites, and tattoos. Everyone was groggy; my parents thought we were lazy teenagers.

"What do you have to be tired about? All you boys did was fish yesterday," my mom said as she ironically placed the platter of bacon on the table.

"We stayed up too late playing Monopoly," Brian said in a half-truth. We had indeed played as we waited for my parents to fall asleep.

"Well that's your own fault. Don't think you're getting out of cutting the grass today."

If the Smokies had caught us, the Pressed-Ham-On-The-Police-Station-Window episode could have been avoided.

Makin' a Livin'
1990
16 years old

Parents are now going with their kids on job interviews! What are we trying to raise here, veal? Brian and I went on our first job interview when we were eleven years old, without our parents, or a ride for that matter. My mom and dad pointed us in the right direction and let us figure out life on our own.

"What do you do at a job interview?" I asked my dad.

"Tell the boss that you are better than everyone else; and maybe don't wear your cutoffs."

Our dad was always a bounty of wisdom. Departing for college, my mom insisted he share with us his best fatherly advice. All he could come up with on the spot was "Wear condoms." He received a nice slap across the chest as we drove away. In hindsight, this was actually solid advice. Other advice included how to shoot a moving target with a shotgun, how to burn a hornet's nest without completely getting your ass tore up, and that a rabbit always circles back to its original location when being chased by beagles.

Brian, Ray, and I were young capitalists and therefore not afraid to work on and off the clock to make a little dough. We had our regular jobs in construction, cutting grass, lifeguarding, gas pumping, selling raccoon pelts, and putt-putt golf course security. Our stolen earnings always tasted sweeter.

Our parents proudly instilled a solid work ethic in all three of us. They took pride in the fact we bought our own cars, clothes, fishing gear, and the endless supply of ammo needed to get us through a weekend. Sure, it upset my mom that we were skinning wild and occasionally not so wild animals for gas money. However, we didn't drink or do drugs, and the boys in blue had not knocked on her door in years. She was a glass half-full kind of woman.

Most of our regular scores were seasonal. In summer, we were watermelon farmers. Close to Ray's house were large fields of a variety of crops. We would monitor the melons for perfect ripeness and make sure we planned our harvest before the rightful owner planned his. Once they were ripe, it was time to put on our green jeans, or camo jeans and black shirts in this case.

The quickness and simplicity of this heist was its beauty. We would all three get in a pickup truck fitted with plywood walls — designed by Ray — that looked just like real melon farmer's. Under the cover of darkness we would approach the farm at around 50 mph. At this point the driver, always Ray, would slide the truck into neutral and kill the engine and lights. I have yet to meet anyone else who had an official getaway driver at sixteen. The truck would hit the embankment at full speed, he would skillfully stick the landing, and then roll the truck another 100 or so feet into the middle of the field; a few melons always lost their lives in the process.

Once stopped, we would leap from the truck and collect our bounty. When the truck was piled as high as humanly possible, Ray would lock the hubs into four-wheel drive and creep out of the field in blackness. After we hit the road, the lights went on and we slid back to his house.

The next day we took back roads to the place we always fenced our contraband, Buckhorn Landing. Buckhorn was a very exclusive club for white trash, a country-country club if you will. I am not sure what the membership dues were, but it couldn't have been much more than a sleeve of Copenhagen, a jumbo bag of barbeque pork rinds, or a set of old Chrysler tires. While working at this elitist joint, I witnessed a variety of refined acts including but not limited to: a preacher getting a beat down with a golf club over a game of horseshoes, a man pulling a pistol after a heated barbeque debate, and a drunk man drowning after going boating with a one-foot hole in his boat. Needless to say, my mom hated the place; she did not like the idea of us breathing in all that second-hand singlewide.

Although ignorant hillbillies, these folks knew a deal when they saw one. With our volume and low operational expenses we were able to pass our savings on to our customers with half-priced melons. We grossed around $500 a truckload and were fishing by noon. In October we'd repeat this play with pumpkins.

Come December, there wasn't much legal or illegal work for us, and our coffers were drying up. We were discussing our lack of options in the kitchen when my mom walked in.

"Can you believe they want $80 for a Christmas tree down at Piggly Wiggly?" she complained. "That is just ludicrous; this Christmas thing is getting way out of hand."

Thank you, Marilyn! We now had our Christmas job.

Christmas trees sell for a mint. The plan was the same as the melons, except harvesting them and loading them was a bit more difficult. Obviously, we couldn't use a handsaw and cut them down one by one, and a chainsaw might sound a little suspicious. Ray had "acquired" a large bush hook from a fireman's truck; it was a large axe-like device with a blade about a foot long. Using a bench grinder and a whetstone Ray made it sharp enough to shave with. The second problem was that the trees were so bulky you could only load a few on the back of a truck before they fell overboard. We remedied this with sets of bungee cords wrapped around the limbs of each tree.

We would only get one shot at this job so we brought two trucks and one full-sized van to make it count. The farm was down a rural dirt road; good for avoiding the cops, but bad for potentially getting your ass shot by a gun-wielding redneck. There would be two pullers and one chopper. The pullers, Brian and Ray, would jump and grab the top of the tree and pull it over, exposing the trunk of the tree. I would run up with the bush hook and let it eat. Either through superior bush hook technology, adrenaline, or the channeling of Paul Bunyan, I was able to take each tree down with one chop. We packed them tight and used ropes and come-alongs to keep them secure.

Then greed got the best of us. We wanted one more — we wanted Big Pappa. Big Pappa was three times the height of the other trees and we figured it would fetch a hefty price. The only problem was it was 20 feet from the owner's rusted singlewide.

Safety tip: A rusted singlewide trailer on a dirt road in rural Georgia is packing heat — always has, always will.

Regardless, the tree was worth the risk.

Once we figured out how to get a clean shot at the base, it took several chops to make it through the trunk. So far, so good. However, when the tree fell, the action started. It must have been the tree farmer's favorite tree. It was tied up to a good-ole-boy security system which was comprised of lots of strings, bells, and empty PBR cans. The racket woke the man. It was go time. No need for a meeting; we all went into a full sprint, dragging Big Pappa with cans and bells behind us like a newlywed's car. We were almost to the truck when we heard the door open.

"What the hell is goin' on out thar?" the man slurred in his saggy, whitey not-so-tighties — possibly the precursor to Calvin Klein's boxer briefs.

As he went back inside to grab his gun, we hoisted the great tree to the back of one of the trucks. Large plumes of red dust flew behind our three vehicles, and as we reached the first turn we heard gunshots in the distance.

We had hocked them all by 11:00 a.m. and made around $1,500, with Big Pappa bringing in $120 alone. Our biggest score yet. In hindsight, $1,500 might not have been worth dying for, but rational behavior wasn't one of our strong suits.

Our parents thought us the perfect sons when we brought each of them the pick of the litter. Nothing says "Jesus' birthday" quite like giving your parents a hot Christmas tree to put the loot under.

Egging the Principal's Wife
1990
16 years old

High school was an awkward time in our lives. The late 80's and early 90's were the heyday of janked up haircuts — all of which landed on at least one of us. As was par for the varsity football team, I had a sleek #39 shaved into my head each fall.

The football scene interested me more than the actual game of football — letterman's jackets, pep rallies, the smell of fresh grass, piping hot corndogs, and stale urine wafting from under the bleachers. Football was on a short list of things I could choose to do as a heterosexual white male. To detour from these norms would tell the McCarthy patrol that you were gay, a Commie, or a Yankee.

Physically I had the right tools for the sport, but I was way too rational and soft to be worth a damn. The pre-game Lombardi speeches about these being the "best days of our lives" did not whip me into a steroid rage as intended, but rather left me depressed and anxious for my future. I was relatively broke, lived in my parents' basement, had a $500 car, was stuck in a hopeless rundown between second and third base with my God-fearing girlfriend, and therefore had been banking on life picking up a notch after Bremen Blue Devil football.

My dad, always the coach, attributed my lack of football prowess to my cushy home life. "Your life's too easy for you to be a real ball player," he philosophized. He would then fade into a recruitment daydream and mumble as he walked away, "Man, if you boys had been born in the Projects, now that's something I'd like to see." My dad knew that nothing would kill a kid's football career faster than having middle-class parents. No hunger.

Many kids get arrested during their high school years, but few actually get arrested in the middle of class. There ain't really a way to sugarcoat this story; we pegged the Principal's wife with eggs at point blank range as she leisurely walked the school track with a friend.

I'm not sure why we always turned to eggs as our weapon of choice. Yes, they're affordable and delicious, but it seems like we would have mixed it up a little more.

We were just coming off summer break, which was always a rough transition for us. We'd been running wild for two or three months, and to be abruptly thrown into a domesticated situation was tough. After shooting thousands of rounds of ammo a day, building Mad Max vehicles, and running from gun-brandishing good ole boys during the summer, school life was a bit slow.

Like a junkie trying to get a fix, Brian, Ray, and I were numb to our everyday shenanigans. Stealing brackets out of the bookshelves to watch the librarian get buried under a mountain of books, shooting innocent kids with homemade paperclip guns, and stealing Cokes out of every machine in the building didn't do it; we needed the real smack. Our healthy fear of the law had foolishly eroded, and our concepts of consequences no longer registered in our psyches. Not a good combination.

It was a pleasant fall day and the three of us, along with a couple of girls, were loitering in the parking lot.

"This sucks, we need to do something," Brian yawned, obviously implying something destructive.

"We could egg something," I suggested, shrugging my shoulders at the lameness of my own idea.

"Yeah, I guess we could. I was kind of hoping for something else," Brian said as he rubbed his chin, his trademark deep thought gesture.

"Hell, let's just egg the next person who walks by," Ray said, trying to impress the girls. "Let's get some eggs, walk down there and start pelting those ladies on the track."

"I'll drive — you buy," Ray told Brian as he jumped in the truck.

I stayed behind with the girls, which would be considered one of the only normal activities I did as a 16-year-old boy. Brian and Ray went to People Pleaser, the convenience store located right next to school. They purchased two dozen eggs — eight apiece — were they planning on baking a quiche afterwards? As I came to find out, we would end up using all 24 in less than 30 seconds of stupidity.

When Brian and Ray made it back, we ditched the girls and snuck behind the bleachers to plan our attack.

"What do you think?" I asked.

"Light up the next person who walks by," Ray answered, obviously itching for a fix.

"Wow Ray, you really put a lot of brain power into that elaborate plan," Brian retorted.

"Bite me, dumbass!" Ray snapped.

"Works for me," I said.

"Me too, just messing with you, Ray," Brian laughed.

Our victims were slowly approaching. Ray glanced out through the holes in the concrete stands. "It's Nancy Thomas," he cried. As luck would have it, Mrs. Thomas was our Principal's wife. Mr. Thomas was a legend. On one occasion when a student pulled a fire alarm as a joke, he announced over the intercom that the guilty person "better give yer heart to God because yer ass is mine." He was old school and we dug it. Regardless, a plan was a plan, no matter how ill-conceived.

They walked aggressively and both resembled the husky lady on *The Goonies*. When they reached us, we started lobbing the eggs up and over the thirty-foot stands. This was a difficult shot. Unfortunately, no one delivered a miracle shot like Brian's rock at the train or Ashley's Money Shot. We did nick and spray them and make them do a little *Flashdance*, but no real kill shot. Not from this vantage point anyway.

"Ambush!" Brian yelled.

This is where stupid set in. In our defense, we should have been gradually introduced back into captivity after summer break. We were now at our own school, in broad daylight, egging the Principal's wife from less than twenty feet. My mind went blank as adrenalin bitch-slapped my remaining common sense.

We pounced in unison. They unsuccessfully tried

to block the rapid-fire baby chickens coming at them in threes. Unlike a rock, you cannot really block an egg; you end up with the shell in your hand and the yolk and whatever you call the white part of the egg on your face. There was screaming, which slapped us back into reality.

What had we done?

It was giddy-up time. Twenty-four eggs were launched and now dripping off two innocent, but dangerously powerful women. Once in the truck, we debriefed our temporary lapse in judgment.

"I don't think that was the smartest thing we've ever done," I said, clearly irritated by our collective stupidity.

"You might be right," Brian replied solemnly.

"Do you think they saw us?" Ray asked.

"Well, we were standing directly in front of them when we threw the last dozen," I snapped.

"Good point," Ray said.

"Well, they *were* shielding their faces," Brian offered hopefully.

"Bit of a reach, don't you think?" I said.

"Yeah."

Several days went by. Nothing. Our confidence built as each day passed. Four days later, we had moved on. Mrs. Thomas and the Bremen P.D. had not.

It was fifth period and we were in American History. I had an after lunch coma setting in and couldn't keep my eyes open. There was a knock at the door; I looked up. I saw the blue shirts and badges through the narrow pane of reinforced glass. Brian, Ray, and I quickly shared the "Oh shit!" look. We played it cool; they were not necessarily there for us, although no other students had sweat running down the crack of their ass.

I went through a quick inventory of all of our recent bad deeds; where was Santa Claus when I needed him? The lunchroom tacos must have been drugged because it actually took me several minutes to remember the egging incident.

They entered the classroom and split into mini-SWAT teams of two and went straight to Brian and Ray. This was not going to end well. Neither of them put up a fight, and Bremen's finest cuffed them right at their desks. The straight kids were frozen in their chairs and were clearly more frightened than Brian and Ray.

It was odd that they had not slapped the cuffs on me. As they led the two convicts out of the classroom, the officer in charge stared me down and nodded his head. Was I off the hook? I doubted it. For the next thirty minutes the rest of the class kept stealing glances at me in anticipation; everyone figured they had gone back to the car to get the third pair of cuffs. Inexplicably, they never returned.

Brian and Ray were taken downtown. Come to find out, Brian was right — Mrs. Thomas and her walking partner had indeed been blinded by the egg onslaught and missed my identifiable #39 haircut. The cops had to rely on video camera evidence obtained from the convenience store to track us down. Very *CSI* by Bremen standards. This explained why I had not been cuffed; I was not on the videotape.

The cops were not stupid — well maybe some were, but not all of them. They knew we travelled in threes and figured they could sweat out a confession from Brian and Ray. Yeah, right — the two of them made the Mafia and their Omerta looked like a bunch of gossiping schoolgirls. Once I heard this was the plan, I knew I was safe. And that I would owe them one.

Our parents were dumbfounded. Even though I was technically in the clear, Mom continued to grill me. "Tell me again. Why were you not arrested?" She figured Brian and Ray were serving time for the crime and did not like the idea of me getting off scot-free. She could tell I was a little stressed by the event and in a quiet talk away from everyone I told her the entire story. Although Mom didn't physically keep close tabs on us, she did emotionally — especially on me. I was always more emotionally complex than Brian. If I were self-righteous or insecure I could spin this today into how "deep" or "philosophical" I was, but really it just meant I was always fighting off a nervous tick of one kind or another.

Although most teenagers are insecure, I was paralyzed by it — odd, considering regularly-scheduled felonies didn't seem to bother me. My hair, color of underwear, type of deodorant, buying condoms, school bathrooms, or the fact that I was taller than the asshole seniors on the football team all sent me into spasms. I would shove my size 12 feet into size 10 British Knights in hopes of being fashionable and decreasing my L-shaped profile. On one occasion in the fifth grade, one of the girls in class told me that Brian had the nicest butt in school (a remark once repeated by one of my girlfriends in high school — bitch). The rest of the day was a write-off as I panicked about my zit-covered deformed ass.

This was the last time our parents had to step up with bail money. The next time bail money would be needed we would be 24 years old and it would be waived after Brian's hilarious drunken rendition of *Roxanne* a la Eddie Murphy in *48 Hours*.

Brian and Ray were sentenced to some serious

community service. I tagged along and helped out as I did feel guilty. Plus, what the hell was I going to do by myself for a month? They'd been given the task of gathering every aluminum can from every ditch in Bremen and placing them in a warehouse for recycling.

We must have had some kind of short-term memory defect. Spending hours in the hot sun, our minds began to wonder.

"How much you reckon these cans are worth?" Ray asked.

The wheels of delinquency started to turn and we schemed together a plan to take all the cans, recycle them ourselves, and keep the dough. If not for our hard work, they wouldn't have had the cans in the first place, or so the logic went.

We were rational enough, however, to let things cool down before attempting the heist. Ray took the warehouse key and copied it at a small roughneck store off the beaten path. After several weeks, we started to craft a more detailed plan.

Logistically, the heist was difficult. We would need to move an entire warehouse of cans, a month's worth of collecting, in one night and cash them in before anyone realized they were missing. In addition, the aluminum recycling station was 30 minutes away and only open one Saturday a month.

Trucks were needed. Ray and Brian both had trucks and we borrowed Ray's dad's full-sized pickup. It was great that we had three trucks, but even all three wouldn't put a dent in the amount of cans we had to move. It was time to get the teenage white B.A. Baracus to work.

Ray grabbed his welder and a bunch of scrap metal

from one of the many sheds at his house. We began erecting tall frames, which extended each truck bed upward for ten to fifteen feet. I'm not sure the exact height, but Ray made it exactly as high as a semi, thus preventing any unnecessary power line debacles. The structures were ingenious; they had all types of cross-bracing which even allowed us to climb on them.

The heist would take place on a Friday night. We drove the trucks to the warehouse and parked them in the dark. I was jogging in maximum stealth mode, crouched like a ninja. Smack! I ran shin first into a cable strung across the road and landed flat on my face. Brian and Ray were laughing so hard they didn't even help me up. Once we got a hold of ourselves, we entered the shed using our key, breaking the lock upon departure to fake a B&E.

Over the next several hours we ran bags of cans between the warehouse and the trucks. We were all dripping with sweat in the Georgia darkness. Once all three trucks were full, we pulled out. The first load made a nice dent in the stocks, but we would need to return twice more to empty the shed completely. The massive pile of cans was being staged in a field behind Ray's house.

Construction of the truck frames began at seven p.m., and we had six loads in the field with three on the trucks by six a.m. It was two hours until the recycling depot opened and we needed a break; we were exhausted. We cooked a dozen delicious eggs over our campfire — who knew you could eat them? This one-hour respite around the campfire meant we had not officially lied to our parents about camping out that night.

We needed to fence these hot cans fast. We took back roads the entire way to the depot and were waiting at the gates with the first load when the station operator, who looked as if he just walked off the set of *Trainspotting*, opened the gates at eight a.m. He quickly weighed our load and paid us out. By noon we hocked the remaining six mega-loads of cans to our new best friend. He never asked where we acquired the mountain of aluminum cans, there were no cameras, and he never even asked our names.

All in all, we raked in around $800. Factoring out the time we spent collecting the cans, we made roughly $16-$17 an hour. Not bad money for 1990.

There might be a moral to this story, but I have no damn clue what it is.

The Summer of Gun Powder
1991
17 years old

Society is coddling its teenagers too much nowadays. Parents are threatening teachers for grades, coaches for playing time, and occasionally offing a cheerleader to make room for their little princess. Are they planning to help their kid put a condom on for the first time? Instead of cocooning our kids in Bubble Wrap, we should give them unlimited amounts of gunpowder, stand back — and here is where the magic and faith part of parenting comes in — and let them grow up into well-adjusted adults.

I'll grant you there are some real short-term risks to the anti-Bubble Wrap parenting style. However, the longer-term risks are even greater. Yeah, your little Trevor might never get stitches, but at some point in his life he might run into a heavy situation a time-out won't solve.

Maybe Brent will score straight A's all through school, but if the thought of making a B- makes him shit his pants, that's no good either. Or, Mr. Perfect Teeth Cody might be so frightened of failure that he never takes a gamble in his whole life and ends up a pathetic excuse for a man; one who has to call AAA to change his tire. Taking risks is the spine of America. We were founded by the world's all-star team of swash-buckling lunatic entrepreneurs. Can you imagine our country if our forefathers had been scared to let it hang out? Hell, we'd still be a third world country.

At seventeen, our parents thought of us as adults as they were unaware of our day-to-day activities. Given the people and places we frequented, had we needed protection, it was not the type of thing they could offer. We became our own protectors and looked after our parents as they had us. Dad could handle himself, but if anyone so much as gave Mom a bad look, we were on them like green flies to doodoo. Raise your voice, cut her off in traffic, say anything negative, or if your dog made the unfortunate mistake of biting her, it would be taken care of before sunrise. We made no apologies for this behavior, nor did Mom ask for one.

Our parents did not have our extracurricular activities laid out in a spreadsheet — maybe we missed our chance to be piano virtuosos. It was better to entertain ourselves with pipe bombs than be the neurotic stressed out mess that we see in today's 18 year olds. I think.

If you liked blowing shit up, rural Georgia was the place to be in 1991. The Summer of Gunpowder was far and away the most moronic and dangerous season of our hooligan years. Brian, Ray, and I had been burning and blowing up stuff our entire lives in a personal arms race to out-do ourselves. It was not until the FBI showed up that we knew we had reached our full potential.

I've described our Snap-n-pop bombs, landmines, and hand grenades. Our potato guns would have made NASA proud. Tennis balls filled with gunpowder worked well for blowing up mailboxes, and if that didn't work we'd just hit the box with 50-pound rocks at 75 mph until it shattered. These amateur devices were no longer doing it for us; we needed to take it up yet another notch.

To expand our talents we'd need more gunpowder. With our summer jobs and heist money fattening our pockets we had some dough to play with, but were still not sure how to go about buying bulk gunpowder.

The three of us pooled fifty dollars and drove down to the local militia headquarters, which moonlighted as an arms dealer. The store looked as if it was preparing for some sort of *Red Dawn* invasion, where Russians somehow, and for no apparent reason, attack a rural community in the middle of nowhere to capture Aunt Margaret's classified peach cobbler recipe. There were the usual dead animal heads hanging on the walls, and everyone was dressed in head-to-toe camo. I was not sure why they wore camo to shoot targets in the dirt, but I was afraid to ask.

There was a wall of plastic containers similar to the protein powder ones that muscle head guys have on top of their fridges. I counted twenty or so different kinds of powder in a variety of sizes.

"Ray, just grab one, pay for it, and let's get the hell out of here," I whispered as I ducked behind the automatic weapon rack to avoid eye contact with the shopkeeper.

Ray had other plans.

"Excuse me, sir," Ray lathered on his deepest southern drawl, which was virtually effortless considering he talked this way all the time. "What can you tell me about this here gunpowder?"

What the hell was he doing? He was not being stealth; he was chewing the shit with the shopkeep like they'd shared tours in 'Nam.

"Sure thing. Whatcha lookin' for, Son?" Yo Samity Sam asked.

"What are my options?"

"Well, powder comes in a variety of forms and each burns differently."

"Which is the fastest?"

"Well, that would be the FUBAR 280 which is designed for fast firing M-16 army caliber assault rifles," Yo Samity Sam intoned.

"We'll take it!" Ray replied a little too eagerly.

We walked out with three gallons of the fastest burning gunpowder on the market; we made the Hindenburg look like a pillow fight. The sheer volume of explosive powder in the car made us all giddy.

It took a few iterations to actually perfect a pipe bomb. Once we had it down we blew up trees, abandoned cars, not so abandoned cars, and tanks full of gas.

This all took place around the always sophisticated Buckhorn Country-Country Club. The neighbors began to get suspicious when they had to rehang their pictures each weekend after an explosion knocked them down. We went through two gallons of powder before it was time for the finale. We put the remaining gallon of powder into a home-made cannon.

Ray welded the cannon from the end of a 12-inch galvanized steel pipe. Next we needed a projectile, which we argued about for some time. It had to be heavy and fit the cannon as snug as possible. We finally settled on a stone from a river we found after trying a few hundred others. It fit perfectly with a large rag used as wadding. To really get fancy we ran wires from a car battery to ignite the cannon instead of the usual fuse. Ray's idea of course.

When it came time for detonation, we had no idea how far the 20-pound stone would fly, but wanted to find out. We aimed the cannon across Lake Buckhorn, which equaled roughly a half mile.

Everyone hid behind something sturdy just in case the rock got lodged and the entire thing blew chunks. Ray brought out the car battery. "Three. Two. One!" Ray hollered as he put the wires to the battery. Nothing. He tried again. Nothing. Again. Nothing. And just as we all relaxed our sphincters it went off as if Hiroshima had relocated to a small, white trash, rural neighborhood. The concussion left me short of breath, and with all the smoke I thought I was floating in the clouds of Heaven: I guess the fact that it was Heaven should have tipped me off that I wasn't actually dead. Although we didn't discuss Hell in detail at Sunday School, I've always imagined it as a large public airport bathroom with the Beach Boys, arguably the whitest of all bands, playing over the intercom. The explosion was much larger than anticipated, and we will probably all have hearing problems later in life. It took three days for the ringing in my ears to let up.

All three of us peered through the smoke hoping to catch the stone during splash down. I thought I saw something toward the horizon, but I wasn't sure. We waited for a splash that never happened. Our stone cannon ball had cleared the lake, apparently quite easily. There was not even any movement in the trees beyond the lake. How far had it gone? Did it make it to the next neighborhood a mile away? We weren't sure, but sure weren't hanging around to find out. Before we could skedaddle, though, we saw a pickup truck coming our way.

Ray's dad Fred was a hell of a man. He was half Cherokee, and it looked as if you could strike a match off his face. His hands were those of a man who had been breaking down diesel engines for almost half a century. He always gave us a wide berth, and I can't remember him ever telling us not to do something. He figured if we got hurt we most likely deserved it, and the best he could hope for was that we would learn from our stupidity.

Ray was the youngest of seven kids; the only love he got was tough love. For the first five years of his life he slept on a blow-up raft. My friends now have an entire room full of supplies to help their baby sleep. Their little nugget even has a vibrating bed and a wave machine, despite the fact they live in Nebraska and his parents have never even seen the ocean. It's like riding an enormous feather-stuffed dildo at the beach. Who wouldn't fall asleep after that?

Fred drove up in his blue GMC pickup. He didn't say a word as he got out of the truck, picked up our 70-pound cannon and demolition toolbox like they were feathers, and proceeded to walk toward the dock. Once at the end, he threw all the materials in the lake. As he stalked by us he said one sentence: "I don't want to ever talk about this again," got back in his truck, and drove back to the house.

Had this been any other man on the planet, his comment would have carried zero weight, but not with Fred. If he said something, he meant it, and he meant it for a good reason. We did not know what was going down, nor did we want to.

118

Years later we found out that the FBI had been asking around about us. They didn't know who we were specifically, but asked Fred about any knowledge of some pipe-bomb building kids. He covered for us and then took care of business before they returned.

I'm happy we didn't get caught by the FBI, but I'm also thankful they came around when they did. Had we not been on rural Georgia's most wanted list, we most likely would have maimed or killed ourselves.

How we escaped jail or a casket after such idiotic behavior is beyond me, but I'm grateful to any and all natural and supernatural beings who helped out, especially Fred.

There are many morals to this story. But if I need to spell them out for you, you're probably too dumb to read a book in the first damn place.

Joy Ride

1992

17 years old

Bo and Luke jumped rivers in the General Lee, the most racist car on television; we tried it with a 19-foot Crown Vic.

It all started at the local Veterans of Foreign Wars (VFW) juke joint, otherwise known as a Legion. Brian, Ray, and I were paid to collect the cover charge and check everyone's I.D. We were only 16; I'm not sure how we got the gig. Maybe we blended in better than I would now like to think. It seemed to make sense at the time.

Our parents only allowed it because we would be graduating in a few months and moving out anyway. They merged us into full independence, unlike the freshmen girls at college who ended up on the cover of *Girls Gone Wild*. Different than today, our parents didn't go with us to register for classes, harass our teachers, pick our apartment, or show us how to buy groceries. A smile and a wave was all we got as we drove off from the house. Well, my dad was definitely smiling; Mom seemed a little sad.

The VFW was jammed with rural Georgia's finest. I never saw any minorities at the bar; I guess they were either excused from foreign wars or just not invited to the crappy redneck after-party. All the men drove trucks, sported mullets, and proved their strength by lifting truck transmissions with one arm. Jeff Foxworthy could have sat in the parking lot and written a book each weekend. The women also rocked mullets or perms or both, and looked like tanned leather in heels. If we watched closely, we could even see the occasional lady dipping Copenhagen — it was a real classy joint. When the bar closed there was usually a fight or two in the parking lot, and we'd comb through the rocks looking for loose change and jewelry when they were finished.

In a scene straight out of *Wild Kingdom*, we would watch the old wildebeests do their mating dance each night. Their dancing looked like someone had stabbed a drunken stork with a pitchfork. It was a disgusting sight, but not watching was out of the question. As the night wore on, pairs were formed; the shallow end of the gene pool expanded, and once again Darwin was proven wrong.

It didn't take long for a plan to hatch out of this weekend party dipped in ass. On the night of Operation Joy Ride, we carefully observed and examined all the patrons. We had the herd picked apart and the most vulnerable beast marked.

Sheila was a character. She liked to dance, drink, smoke, dip, fight, and more than anything, screw. Her hair looked like sun-bleached bailing twine. The jeans she squeezed into Saturday night ought to be in the denim hall of fame. Her perfume was a cross between trashy and sophisticated; one jelly jar of Southern Comfort would tip the scales in either direction. Sheila came to the bar looking for a good time, and she always seemed to find it in one position or another.

This was 1991, when a "cougar" was still a large cat, not a woman who is hot, old, and preys on young men. Even so, Sheila couldn't be categorized as a true cougar; she scavenged as opposed to hunted, and the age of her prey was irrelevant. She might be better described as a sexually aggressive hyena. Sheila was also married; a fact that didn't slow her down one bit, but is a very important element to this story. I'm not sure what type of man would have married Sheila — I never met him. I always assumed he was at home with their six kids (of which, rumor has it, only three resembled him in any way — the six-foot-six red head being the most obvious outlier).

Sheila moved in for the kill around one a.m. She stalked a severely inebriated cowboy who was stumbling toward his truck. In this neck of the woods drunk driving was a sport; mothers were not only not MADD, they were usually riding bitch. That girl moved fast; I am not sure what she whispered to the cowboy, but it sure as hell worked. She was a pack of one, and within thirty seconds she was jumping into his truck, leaving her own beautiful boat behind. I hope he dipped himself in bleach the next morning. Our new ship was a white and rust colored Crown Vic with a 4.6 L V8 under the hood. We waited until three a.m. to make our move.

The parking lot had been empty for almost two hours and only a few cars passed on the road. To avoid the lights, we entered the woods and took the long way around to our target parked in the back end of the lot. The plan was straightforward: Ray would use his Slim Jim to break in and hotwire the boat. Brian and I would egg him on to do what he did best — drive like the illegitimate child of Dale Earnhardt and Richard Petty if they were able to procreate in some freaky man-on-man action.

Brian and I waited in the woods. Ray slid the Slim Jim between the window and door and then looked up in surprise.

"It's unlocked," he whispered.

This was going to be easier than we expected. We all three piled in and Ray ducked under the dash with his pliers and flashlight. He came up ten seconds later, which would have been fast even for him.

"The keys are in it."

It was meant to be.

Brian and I were riding shotgun; no one was demoted to the backseat on this trip.

"You boys better buckle up," Ray ordered as the V8 came to life.

Although we ran amuck in almost every way, self-enforced safety standards like this kept us alive. Another one that really paid off was not aiming loaded guns at each other.

I love two-wheel drive. Ray mashed the pedal like it owed him something and dog-whipped three tight doughnuts. Captain Ahab then slid it out of the last doughnut cocked at 45 degrees from the direction in which we were traveling. I think this is called "drifting" in one of those crappy car movies where the manly men drive around in souped-up Honda Civics. He took this path all the way to the street, where the Crown Vic grabbed the asphalt, sending a strong torque through the car. I felt a brief stir of panic in my stomach until I saw the grin on Ray's face, which basically said, "Yo, Nate, chill the fuck out. I got this bitch under control. Kick back and enjoy the ride."

It took a while for the tires to completely catch up to the car, but once we were up on plane we were doing around fifty.

"Stand on it!" Brian ordered.

Brian was always guilty of daring Ray, and Ray was always guilty of taking him up on it — not that he needed any encouragement. The Crown Vic was closing in on triple digits. The shell of the car was floating off the frame in a side-to-side motion. Driving this fast down rural paved roads was extremely dangerous with diminishing thrill; we needed dirt roads to maximize the thrill while minimizing the risk of death and dismemberment.

A car passed us in the oncoming lane. It wasn't a cop, but it gave us a good excuse to run from somebody. Ray slammed on the brakes in order to hit a hard right down the pipeline.

Our ship was on dirt. Ray must have been born on a dirt road; he was the Beethoven of red clay. The pipelines in Georgia are a large network of dirt roads and trails most NASCAR drivers cut their teeth on in their early teens. The road we'd chosen was more of a dirt bike trail, but Sheila's boat managed to fit. We'd driven the trail before, and Ray knew which trees we could and could not run over. It didn't take long to lose both side mirrors. Our chauffeur clipped a few abandoned cars and 50-gallon drums, digging inch-deep furrows down each side. All four quarter panels were now concave, and the front windshield had a spider web cracking up from the bottom right. The ventilation in the car was poor, and I was starting to get a dust headache when Ray yelled, "Here comes the river!" It might be truthfully described as a large creek, but we called it a river to make it sound more impressive in the event that we cleared it.

"I think we can make it!" screamed Ray over the rocks and debris hitting the car. Negative, Ghost Rider. The pattern was full.

Small hills flanked the river making nice ramps for dirt bikes and four wheelers; I doubt they were designed with oversized speeding cars in mind. The car went airborne, and we heard the telltale whine of the wheels free spinning in the open air. Unlike the Dukes, Waylon Jennings was not playing music in the background or delivering the brief narration before the commercial break.

It was dark, so I'm not sure how high we were, but I think not being able to see the ground made it seem even higher. The landing was far from Mary Lou Retton and nothing like the cars that fly horizontal on TV. It dropped like that gangly white guy who fought Tyson. We hit headfirst into the upcoming bank, which subsequently shoved the back end into the opposite bank, effectively bridging the creek with the car. The seat belts had done their job and Ray was gassing Sheila's Crown Vic to get it unstuck. A smooth ZZZZZzzzzzzzzzzZZZZZZZzzzz is all we heard.

"I think the ride is over," Ray said as he unfastened his seatbelt.

We leaped from the car, now five feet off the ground. Our boat was dry-docked and bookended by the river banks. Even with all three of us pushing on the car, we could not get it to budge.

"It was fun while it lasted," Brian laughed.

As we started walking back, the story grew and grew each time it was relived. It took us 45 minutes to get back to the bar, find our own truck, and head home.

The beautiful Crown Vic was left right where it landed; it would be discovered the next day by whoever took the trail first. We weren't nervous about the owner trying to track us down. It would be hard for Sheila the Hyena to explain to her husband why her car had been left at the bar and subsequently found suspended above a river five miles down a motorbike trail. I'm not sure what story she told him, but it never came back to us.

The moral of the story is this: If you are going to cheat on your spouse, do not leave your car at the bar unlocked with the keys in the ignition when 16-year-olds who believe *The Dukes of Hazzard* is a documentary are running the door.

The Slingshot Incident

College

It's impossible to fully describe the noise a stomach makes when hit with a ball bearing going 150 mph; you had to be there, as they say.

Brian, Ray, and I had come home from college for Thanksgiving. It was a beautiful southern fall day; brightly colored leaves welcomed us home while the air smelled like football. We would finally have some decent food and see our families.

Mom continued to lure us home with food to check on us a few times a year. It only took her one glance to know if we had any real issues in our lives. We tried to hide as much as we could from her to prevent her from worrying; the fact that we had been eating only cornflakes and catfish from the pond on campus never came up in conversation.

It was going to be a mellow weekend with some

fishing and hunting. We still had pumpkin pie on our breath when Marla, our sister, got a phone call.

Our poor sister is a separate book by herself, possibly entitled *A Ruined Childhood — The Curse of my Last Name*. That girl got busted doing everything; she even got arrested for spray-painting an abandoned road. She might have caught a little more shit than she deserved after the path her older brothers blazed for her. Her finest high school moment was a basketball game brawl that made the front page of the paper after she broke the star athlete's nose and crippled his dick with a roundhouse kick. It was made funnier by the fact that she is gorgeous, and unbelievably photogenic even during a real life scene from *Road House*. Our parents were so proud.

Marla received a phone call from a Good Samaritan telling her that a group of kids who had their hate-on for her were coming to TP our house. At first we didn't think much of it; we just made fun of Marla and said she should be nicer to the ugly kids at school. A few hours later it dawned on us.

They were attacking our house! Yes, we had been away at college for a year, but we hadn't been killed in a tragic frog gigging accident. This was still our castle and we still demanded the same amount of respect for it, whether we were in town or not. Or perhaps we were bored and looking for an excuse to finally shoot someone with a slingshot. Take your pick.

None of us had ever shot someone with a slingshot. We would have loved to, but opportunities like this do not grow on trees. Although we readily ran up and hit innocent bystanders with eggs from point blank range, shooting someone with a wrist-rocket was something different entirely. Even with our dismantled moral compass we didn't have the heart to jump out and start violently attacking strangers. The shooting would also need to take place in close quarters making it impossible to escape. This was our ultimate fantasy, one that we had all but given up on.

For our dream to come true we would need someone to attack us, something that never happened while we still lived at home. This would remove all responsibility from our actions, "I swear Officer, we were just defending ourselves." All three of us were skilled marksmen with a wrist rocket. Earlier in the day, we shot a few practice rounds at cans in the backyard — it was like riding a bike.

Ordinarily we would just shoot rocks, but for such a special occasion we needed something more deadly, so we'd gone to Wal-Mart. Wal-Mart sold a package of ball bearings specifically designed for our wrist rockets that flew faster and with more power than even a normal marble. Mom knew exactly what we were up to and only shook her head and smiled — she was glad we were home.

The buildup was almost too much to handle. Marla, Brian, Ray, and I stayed up late that night waiting to ambush our prey. The adrenaline wore off eventually and everyone gave up and went to sleep, except Marla. She sat in the window all night believing in the ill will of her schoolmates. I gained a lot of respect for my sister that night. There was no way she was going to let these punks violate our home, and she was more excited than anyone to see her two older brothers and their lunatic friend light up her enemies with balls of pain.

From a deep sleep I was violently shaken awake at three a.m. by Marla.

"They're here!" she whisper-yelled.

"Huh?"

"Wake up, dumbass! Get your slingshot!"

Brian and Ray were already up and dressed. I looked out the window and saw the group within feet of our yard. No time for clothes. We slid out like panthers, me in my spicy weekend boxers and hunting boots. Everyone was in their designated spot when the punks arrived. The three of them each had two rolls of toilet paper. There were two small boys and one Oompa-Loompa-looking girl. Our team was frozen and patient. No need to rush it.

"One, two, three," their leader counted as they reared back to throw their first roll.

It is impossible to throw something straight up without leaving your vitals open. As they rocked on to their back leg and cocked their arms, a glow in the dark bullseye practically appeared on their stomachs.

There were three of us with slingshots; there were three of them — easy math. Each person on our team took the person closest to them. The synchronized stomach opening was a nice touch and was self-explanatory. No formal countdown was needed for our troops. They did it for us.

As the toilet paper was getting ready to leave their hands we simultaneously drilled each of them a new belly button. I'm pretty sure I shot the Oompa-Loompa, but I was too embarrassed to tell anyone. All three took a nasty gut shot to start the night off. They dropped and began yelping in pain. I felt they were being a bit melodramatic, but then again I've never taken a rifle strength ball bearing to the gut, so I shouldn't judge. It made a noise that I can only describe as the sound made when you hit a watermelon with a broom handle.

"They're shooting at us!" the brightest one yelled.

They tried their best to run while humped over in agony. There was no way to prevent the next onslaught. We had tasted blood and were high on our new-found power. Each punk took a few shots to the back as they limped away whimpering. They made it to their car, which also took several shots, resulting in a cracked front windshield.

The car was obviously a stick, and they could not get it together. It started and stopped, hucked and bucked. It sounded like they left the transmission on the road, and they ended up slowly rolling down the hill.

We let them retreat in peace and gave in to hysterical laughter. I was starting to shiver when Marla looked over. "Nathan, are those glow in the dark underwear?"

Going to Graduate

College

D is for diploma and R is for rappelling down a 20-story building at two a.m. to steal such a diploma.

For obvious reasons, this will be the first story I will change names and any damning details to protect our protagonist. I will simply call him Spiderman — no offense to Peter Parker or Stan Lee.

Spiderman was a bright student and could have made all A's with little effort. The only problem was that Spidey also had a nasty party and womanizing habit. It was hard to make it to ethics class when you were exhausted from running half naked from a jealous powerlifter boyfriend two hours earlier.

Brian, Ray, and I had a great college experience despite the fact our high school did little to promote post-secondary education. For Career Day in high school we were encouraged to be truck drivers, air conditioning repairmen, policemen (not us specifically), and everyone's fallback — Marines. Fifteen years later I would volunteer at the same career fair and feel out of place as the only presenter without a weapon.

It only took a few crappy jobs, mine with an organized crime boss, to inspire us to leave town for greener pastures. And let's face it, we had crapped in our own pasture quite a bit by the twelfth grade. Although Ray hated school, he hated the idea of being left behind more, and is now a successful civil engineer instead of a gold medalist in the Redneck Games.

After a brief stint at Georgia Southern University, a college for idiots, we all transferred to the beautiful plains of Auburn University, the best damn school on the planet. All three of us co-oped the entire way through school to make ends meet. Times were tight, but we always seemed to pull something off each time we thought we were going to have to start selling semen to keep the lights on.

The school unknowingly supplied us with cleaning materials, TP, trashcans, the occasional VCR, and student-made pottery dishes for our Ramen Noodles. Once Ray moved in, we went off the grid by poaching all our utilities from the neighbors. A few utility bills were not going to stand in the way of us getting a diploma.

Our parents loved to visit but always found our lifestyle a bit baffling.

"Why do you boys use these huge rolls of toilet paper?" my dad would ask. We usually just told them we got a good deal on it, but that didn't explain away everything.

"Man, you boys have more channels than I do."

"Why do you have so many damn VCRs?"

"Where'd you get a smoke machine from?"

"How do you accidentally blow up your toilet?"

"I don't see how you can live like this," Mom would say worried.

What were they expecting? Our total rent was only $200 a month.

Spidey had been in college for almost a decade at this point, and time was running out. More importantly, he had burned every bridge in town; it was getting harder to go out at night without an uncomfortable run-in with a "date" or a jealous boyfriend. It was time to pull the ripcord.

To graduate from Auburn University you needed a 2.0 G.P.A. Our hero was around a 1.990 with one class and only one final project to go. A D on his final project would bump his GPA up to a 1.995, which would be rounded up to the magic 2.0, and Spidey could get out while the getting was good ('good' defined as somewhat STD-free and still alive).

Spidey knew he was too far behind to legitimately try to pass, and he was nervous. Desperate times called for desperate measures. We were all watching *Lonesome Dove* — this VHS tape and homemade roach-killing blowguns were our only entertainment before we jacked the neighbor's cable. We would pop the tape back in when we were feeling nostalgic. Spidey strode into the room dressed head to toe in black, carrying a set of bolt cutters and 200 feet of rappelling rope lifted from an army barracks three years earlier.

"I'm going to graduate," Spidey declared matter-of-factly as he walked out the door.

If Spidey had worked half as hard doing the projects versus trying to get out of them, he would have graduated four years sooner.

That morning, Spidey Superglued the lock to the back stairwell of a building on campus, preventing it from locking. Under the cover of darkness he made his way to the target building. Once there he sprinted up 20 flights of stairs and climbed up the ladder leading to the roof and open sky. At the top of the ladder a padlocked trapdoor prevented students from doing stupid things on the roof, although I don't think the institution anticipated this level of stupidity. Spidey whipped out his trusty bolt cutters and snapped the lock, placing the pieces in his pocket. These were veteran bolt cutters; they had been around the block a few times.

Once on the roof, with the stars as his guide, he ran to the north end of the building and found a secure anchor. Relying on a standard fishing knot, the only kind he knew, he tied his rope to the air conditioner and threw it over the wall in a previously marked line. Contrary to his moniker, Spidey actually had no idea how to rappel and was just winging it at this point.

He leaned out over the wall and began his descent. Once he reached the twelfth floor he swung into an open window. He knew it would be open because he had opened it earlier that day with a sleight of hand while his professor was explaining how impossible it would be for him to graduate. I guess the teacher did not realize he was talking to a superhero at the time.

He didn't bother to unclip. Once inside he went straight for his target, the teacher's pet's (yes, they still exist in college) final project. This project was most certainly A+

work. He stuffed it in his bag and leaped back out the window and down to the ground. To avoid suspicious security guards, he sprinted back up the 20 flights of stairs and pulled his rope back up to the roof. He then flew back down and back to our house.

We were just getting to the water moccasin scene in *Lonesome Dove* when Spidey entered the house in a full sweat. There was no time for chitchat; he went straight to his room. Over the next three hours he copied the hell out of that project, but was careful enough to make it undetectable in any way.

Once complete, he sprinted to school, up the 20 flights of stairs, rappelled down, put the project back where he found it, rappelled the rest of the way down, ran back up 20 flights of stairs, pulled up his rope, ran down 20 flights of stairs, and ran his ass back home for some well-deserved pancakes.

The next day, to the surprise of the professor, who was a smug Mr. Rogers with a dark brown goatee and ponytail, Spidey turned in his final project just before the deadline. The professor knew something was up, but could not figure what. The project was too high quality to be Spidey's, yet he could not fathom a way to cheat on this type of project. He stared at Spidey over the rim of what would have been considered retro glasses if he was half as cool as he thought he was — Spidey stared back.

The professor did not like it, or maybe he just wanted to get rid of our hero. Either way he gave him a D. The project was A+ quality, if you factor out the plagiarism part. The professor was sending a message to Spidey that he was no fool. Spidey didn't blink: A, B, C, D — he did not give a damn as long as it was not an F.

Until his diploma was surprisingly in his hand, we were never told exactly what had gone down.

I reckon if you are willing to risk your life for your diploma, you deserve it.

The Shit Bomb
– the Greatest Practical Joke
in the History of Mankind

College

You might question the truthfulness of this story, but 25 shit-covered southern belles will tell you it is solidly anchored in two gallons of soupy cow shit.

Brian, Ray, and I considered practical jokes an art form. Our friends and enemies were our canvas, and turds were our medium on more than one occasion. To stay ahead of our competitors each stunt was always one notch better than the last. It was impossible to continue to improve them perpetually; in theory we would reach perfection at some point, and perfection, my friends, was The Shit Bomb.

The Shit Bomb was our tour de force. Not only was the Shit Bomb the greatest practical joke in the history of mankind, it was a metaphor for our entire childhood as we abruptly transitioned into our adult lives. It took all of our best skills and worst morals to craft such a beautiful beast. The three of us were The Shit Bomb, just as The Shit Bomb was us. We cannot relive The Shit Bomb, just as we cannot relive our childhoods.

After this incident I graduated and unfortunately parted ways with Brian and Ray. Despite having not lived in the same country since, or not communicating for months, we are all still brothers and best friends. My departure has always weighed heavy on me, especially when their desperate wives or girlfriends call hoping I might be the one person on the planet to talk them out of opening an underground casino in a house of worship.

As to be expected, my desire to travel baffled my dad. Having graduated at the top of my class and with some solid work experience, I had several job offers — all of which paid more than he was making as a public school teacher and football coach.

"You're going to be a bartender?!?" my dad commented with a squinted face. "You've done some stupid shit in your day, but this has to be up there. But hell, it's your life, just don't send me the bill."

We didn't really fight as he did have a point. I was being a dumb-ass, but at this point he was well aware of my penchant toward illogical behavior.

Mom, on the other hand, understood completely. We've always been the most alike, and therefore the closest. She jokes that it's because I'm her oldest, if only by a few minutes. Although my mom has an adventurous soul, she wasn't able to live out most of her dreams. Given her sketchy childhood, her dream of raising a "normal" family consumed most of her adult life. When I explained my career plan, or lack thereof, she was ecstatic. She ran to the store and bought me the nicest backpack and camera she could find and only asked that I send back plenty of photos.

The Shit Bomb was the climax of a four-year-long practical joke war with our neighbor, Big M. Big M lived above us and was a heavy-footed individual with a black belt in cock-blocking who would have made an excellent stunt double for the late John Candy. You could bring a girl home at any time of the day and Big M. would show up on your couch and eat Cheetos. Even if we called her out on it, she would just laugh and sit there like Chester Cheetah with a slower metabolism. She was truly good-time kryptonite.

I can't say for sure how this particular practical joke war started, but I will outline the significant tactical maneuvers that led up to our masterpiece.

The first incident occurred on a hot spring day. Auburn, Alabama, comes alive in spring with the dogwood trees and daffodils in bloom and the hot southern girls finally starting to show some more skin — including Big M. She refused to wear anything but flip-flops in the spring. If I were her I would have covered my feet; her toes looked like sausages if sausages ate sausages. For some reason we didn't want to know, Big M was drying her mattress in the backyard. Although we shared the duplex, the backyard was ours, or at least we said it was.

"Get yer crab-infested mattress off our yard!" Ray told Big M, who was standing on the upstairs porch. Ray always had a way with words.

"Up yours, Ray!" Big M squawked back in her paper thin sweat pants.

"Move it, or I'll burn it."

143

"You're chicken shit. Our neighbors might notice a bonfire here in the middle of town, dumbass."

Since this was our first year at Auburn, Big M was unaware of the Do not dare Ray Womack under any circumstances rule.

Ray sashayed inside, picked up a jug of lighter fluid and a box of strike-anywhere matches. We tended to always have these two items readily available for just such an emergency. Without a word, he stalked out and sprayed the entire jug of lighter fluid on the mattress, despite the fact that a mattress burns like a hot damn even without the extra help.

"What are you doing?" Big M shrieked from her perch, a safe 20 feet away.

"What do you think I'm doing," Ray said as he backed away.

Without a second thought, Ray stood back and lit the fire with his customary match strike, a thump sending the match flying end over end like a burning paper football. The match would fly lit for about seven or eight feet, always leaving plenty of buffer in case he overdid the Boy Scout juice. The mattress was instantly in flames with black smoke and the smell of ass filling our apartment complex. Come to think of it, maybe this wasn't so much a practical joke as just pure vandalism. Regardless, it's still an important element to this story.

"How ya like them apples," Ray yelled over the crackling flames as he strolled back inside with Big M screaming in the background.

Within seconds a few metal springs and a big black rectangle in the grass was all that was left of Big M's sleeping apparatus. Big M retaliated by putting our furniture out in the yard. We enjoyed the new furniture layout with a cold drink and easily put it back in our house before nightfall.

The second incident was an epic upper-decker. I know the upper-decker is now hip and part of pop culture, but this was 1994 and we'd been performing upper-deckers for years at this point. We didn't read about it on the Internet: we dreamt it up from scratch, which means it's likely we performed the original upper-decker in 1986. We won't be looking for royalties, as I don't believe you can patent taking a dump in the back tank rather than the bowl of a toilet. It takes a skilled plumber and a lot of water to fix this disgusting mess. Upper-deckers were perfect for frat boy parties and made a good distraction while we stole their condiments and CDs.

This particular upper-decker was unique. The traditional deposit was a bit embarrassing to time, which could lead to accidents. It also had certain intestinal limitations.

Auburn's vet school had a variety of animals in the school pastures close to campus. It took a few minutes to find the soupy Grade A caca, but when we did, we filled a five-gallon bucket half-way to the top with Ye Ole Reliable — cow dung. I'm glad they didn't spot us; it would have been uncomfortable to explain why we were stealing a bucket of cow shit.

After Big M went to class, Ray quickly shimmied the lock and we proceeded to the toilet. First we cut off the water to the tank. Second, we flushed the toilet leaving the back tank dry. Next, we poured in the diarrhea. Lastly, we cut the water back on. The water didn't actually come out; the trigger ball was floating on top of the mountain of mud, keeping the water valve closed. We jetted.

Big M usually stopped for a few beers and some wings on her way home from class on Thursdays, and this Thursday was no different. The walls of our place were made of onionskin; we could hear each other fart even through two or three walls. We followed her footsteps above us to the bathroom where we could actually hear her pee; thank God she wasn't dropping a deuce or we might have all died in our own vomit.

When she was done, she flushed the toilet, but a flush is not what she got. She got a slow shit lava flow. After a brief period of confusion, she lifted the back of the tank to see what was going on. Seeing the tank filled to the brim with excrement, not of her own making, she panicked and dropped the lid on the tub, shattering it into several pieces. It didn't take her long to piece together the rest.

"I hate you dickheads!" Big M shouted as she jiggled the handle in an unsuccessful attempt to stop the onslaught of oozing cow shit.

It took her weeks to fully flush out the sewage. She was pissed, but still only managed a weak retaliation that I can't even remember at this point.

Chapter Three of the lead up to The Shit Bomb occurred during our junior year. Believe it or not, I was a very serious student and in the throes of my engineering exams. I couldn't concentrate with Big M's heavy steps and late night drunken debauchery. I was pissed and I wanted to retaliate once my exams were over. She didn't interrupt Brian and Ray's studying, as they didn't give a damn about school. This also meant they had plenty of time on their hands and needed the entertainment of another attack.

"What do you want to do to her, Nate?" Ray asked.

"She keeps me up all the time," I answered.

"Well that's easy enough — car horn," Ray said, implying that I'd been in a classroom too much and had lost all my country street cred.

"Obviously," Brian said.

"Yeah, obviously. I haven't really slept in a few days," I said, making an excuse for my lack of vision.

The car horn was another of our standard moves. We had used this trick dozens of times and it always delivered.

While Big M was at class we broke back into her house and ran speaker wires out our window and up the wall into her bedroom. We mounted under her bed a semi truck horn that Ray kept around for this specific purpose.

The speaker wires were completely hidden, so we had all the time in the world to wait for the perfect night, which inevitably came that Saturday. Big M had hit the bars hard and we heard her stumble into her place around two a.m. We listened as she made a peanut butter and jelly sandwich and watched a little late night *Simpsons*. She wound down in a less than an hour and went to bed. Ray started the clock.

After she had been in bed for thirty minutes, we figured she was good and passed out. Ray brought out the battery and set up his station. Ray had charged the battery in the living room for three days to make sure it was fully topped up.

"I love this trick," Ray said sincerely. "It's like a favorite fishing hole."

Ray then expertly applied the red to the red and black to the black. A car horn has a different sound once it's removed from under the hood, especially a semi horn. It will rattle your teeth. The noise is painful and uncomfortable.

It is so loud and all-encompassing it's impossible to even figure out which direction it's coming from.

Big M immediately began yelling.

"Heeeeeeeeelp! Heeeeeeeeelp!" she screamed as she stumbled and fell into her furniture. "What the fuck is going on, somebody help me!"

The combination of the noise and her inebriation made it impossible for her to get her crap together and even make it out of the room. After falling two or three more times she stumbled out and on to the porch in her sexy PJs that she had no business wearing.

"I hope y'all burn in hell!" she slurred as tears began flowing down her cheeks.

We pretended to be empathetic and stopped the horn. As soon as she had cried herself back to sleep, we laid back into it. This scene repeated itself two or three more times with her finally collapsing in a drunken, sweaty exhaustion in her doorway. With her incapacitated, we retreated to our living room to debrief the episode over some chocolate milk and *Lonesome Dove*. We watched Captain Woodrow F. Call beat the crap out of the scout in slow motion 10 or 15 times.

The next day we broke back in and salvaged our horn, and Big M retaliated with a shaving cream and water balloon attack. Water balloons? Really? This was like following up Pearl Harbor with a game of badminton.

In the end, there can be only one ...

It was the spring of 1998 and graduation was upon us, or at least some of us, as Brian and Ray hung around for a few more years. It was a Wednesday morning, and Brian, Ray, and I were having some of our bulk cereal in the living room and reading *Calvin and Hobbes*, *Popular*

148

Mechanics, and *Money Magazine* respectively. While Brian was engrossed in his scholarly literature, he was also flipping through what little mail we received at the house.

"Here's an invitation to Big M's graduation party."

"It's this Friday night," I responded. "I doubt I'll go."

"Ditto," Ray said with a mouth full of cereal.

"What's she doing after graduation?" I asked.

"I think she got a job in Huntsville or something," Ray answered.

"We'll never see her again," I said without an ounce of sadness in my voice.

"The last time, huh," Brian said as he rubbed his chin.

"Ever," Ray said in a serious tone.

"Ever," I said in agreement.

"Cancel yer classes boys, we've got work to do," Ray told us.

"I'll get the coffee goin'," I said as I gathered up some notepads and my wallet.

It was only seven o'clock in the morning, but it was as if Ray's bootlegged power had shorted and was electrifying the entire room. Everyone was on the same wavelength; no breaks, no girlfriends, no phone calls, no homework, no anything except plan the greatest practical joke in the history of mankind.

With nervous energy and caffeine jacking our veins, all three of us strolled around the room, which was about the size of a medium closet. The brainstorming alone lasted almost half a day. Our legal pads were full of ideas and doodles and we were exhausted. There is only one thing in the world that will revitalize a southern boy and cure all ailments. Hangover, heartbroken, failed a class, syphilis: no matter your illness, a sliced-mild-pickle Byron's Barbeque sandwich will fix it. We each had our usual three with Baked Lays (we were trying to cut calories) and went back to the drawing board.

The sun was starting to set on the plains when we began ranking our ideas. Everyone had ownership over his ideas and fought hard for them, but in the end we had a list of five. In no particular order they were; a shit bomb, steal her car, turn a cow loose in her apartment, electrocute her in her sleep, and shoot her with pellet guns. We had all three been pellet gun snipers earlier in our careers. After much debate we took a vote based on feasibility, impact, and vision. Everyone got a first, second, and third-place vote. The Shit Bomb got all three first place votes. Democracy and destiny had spoken.

We now had two days to come up with the design. Ray and I were both in engineering and Brian knew his way around a cow pasture, so we had the perfect skill set for the task.

Ray brought out the white board. Things were heated but respectful as we argued the merits and dangers of each design. After much discussion, we put the design on paper and we all had a well-deserved drink.

"How much money y'all got?" Ray asked, knowing we were all running on fumes at the end of the quarter. Everyone started digging in couches, wallets, book bags, and desk drawers. All in, we had $28.45.

"I guess that'll have to do," he said as he tallied up what he thought our materials would cost.

Luckily, Home Depot was open 24 hours a day in the off-chance three college students were building a late night shit bomb. We all three walked in with our diagram,

$28.45, and Ray had a few tools with him to double-check our sizing specs.

I feel it's best to not completely sketch out the design of The Shit Bomb. Some kid might copy it, kill his chemistry teacher, and sue me. Basically it was a five-gallon bucket with a spring-loaded shit catapult in the middle. The acceleration was generated using eight strands of double thick surgical tubing, 16 times as strong as one wrist rocket. The shit cockpit was a hard-to-find two-gallon metal mixing bowl. The trigger mechanism was pure genius; it was made out of hinges, nails, and fishing line, and worked somewhat like a mousetrap. Once we had our materials, we strolled home to begin construction.

Construction was difficult. Trying to contain this amount of force yet have it trigger on a feather-touch was no small task. We might have brought it up, but we never seriously considered decreasing the power. After a brief sleep, we woke with fresh brains to give it another go. By noon we had our first prototype.

"I've got butterflies," I confessed.

"Me, too. But I think it's because we're out of food," Ray replied.

"Damn, I hope this works," Brian said. "We're cuttin' it close and I doubt we have time for a plan B."

We used a softball for our first trial, as we figured it weighed roughly the same as two gallons of shit. Cocking the mechanism into place was dodgy; it took two of us to push it down while the other placed the nails in the appropriate hair trigger slots. Imagine setting a mousetrap strong enough to kill a capybara; it was nerve-racking.

"Nathan, get that damn nail in there. My arms are startin' to shake," Ray said.

"I'm goin' as fast as I can, you wuss. I've almost got it."

"Got it!"

All three of us slowly walked away from the bomb. There was some creaking and moaning but nothing exploded. After our hearts slowed down, Ray picked up the fishing line trigger.

"Ready?" Ray asked.

"Please work," I prayed.

"Come on baby, you can do it," Brian added.

"Three, two, one," Ray said as he pulled the string.

Everything occurred so fast it was hard to tell exactly what had happened. The bucket went flying through the air from the whiplash as the thousands of pounds of tension were released. As the bucket hit the ground we scanned the sky for the softball.

"Is it in the bucket?" Brian asked, obviously pissed.

"It's not in here!" I answered as I looked in the contraption that had landed at my feet.

"Weird," Brian said.

THUD.

The softball landed ten feet away from us, having been airborne for what seemed like ten minutes. Our faces lit up like a kid on Christmas who just opened a box with a Red Rider machine gun in it. We all began jumping around and hugging in excitement. Even in our wildest dreams we had not planned on it working as well as it did.

"That sucker's badass," I said.

"Holy shit, holy shit, holy shit," Ray said as he danced the *Cotton Eyed Joe* around the yard.

"We've done it!" Brian said with a double arm pump.

Ray made a few adjustments. One was to build in stop pegs at the top of the bucket that would stop the rocketing bowl at its peak, further slingshotting the contents skyward. He also put some extra weight in the bottom of the bucket to help stabilize it.

"Where are the nails?" I asked.

"That's a good question," Ray answered, puzzled.

"I guess they never came down," Brian philosophized.

"What's say we tie a safety string to them when we do this thing for real. It's all fun and games until we kill Big M."

"Not a bad idea, Nate," Brian said.

The party was only a few hours away and we still had lots to do. After several more trial launches we had this thing down. We were launching the softball a couple of hundred feet in the air. It was a magnificent contraption; we had really outdone ourselves.

The Shit Bomb was not complete; it needed some window dressing. Brian ran behind the ghetto grocery store to steal a box large enough to hold our pride and joy, while Ray and I went to Hallmark and spent our remaining $6.75 on shiny silver wrapping paper, a red bow, and a nice card. The nice card is the part that I feel pushed this joke over the edge and most likely solidified the fact that if we do go to hell, we will not need to wait in line.

We reconvened and went to the school pastures and spent almost 45 minutes finding the cow shit with the perfect viscosity. It couldn't be too dry; it would just bounce off the socialites. If it was too watery, it might not have the firmness needed to reach our desired target area.

"I think I got it," Brian said from down the hill.

Ray and I ran down.

"I think you're right," Ray confirmed, poking it with a stick. "Let's test it out."

Ray had a small pot from our kitchen, which I would like to think we did not reuse, that he used to scoop up the sweet doodoo. He practiced throwing the ammo in a jai alai motion with a rapid stop halfway through the swing. It worked perfectly every time.

"Boys, I think we have our shit," Ray told us as he started filling our bucket.

Although we were able to build something that would have made our engineering professors proud, wrapping a present was beyond our capabilities. A random homely girl walked by our apartment, and Brian dropped a smooth line on her and asked her for help.

"What's in the box?" the girl wondered.

"You don't want to know," Brian answered.

"It's not a dead body, is it?" she inquired.

"I can honestly tell you it is not a dead body," Brian said, as if that made everything better.

"You're right, I don't wanna know," she said as she caught her first whiff of our projectile, which was casually kicking it in the corner.

That girl must have worked in retail. It looked like a perfect shiny metallic box with a removable metallic lid when she finished. We stuck the bow on and signed the card.

"Dear Mandy, we're sorry we could not make it to your graduation party. We've had a lot of fun over the last four years and we will sincerely miss you. Congrats! Brian, Ray, and Nathan"

It was complete, and we had several painful hours to burn. Big M was no longer living above us and had moved across the street into an apartment, possibly for safety reasons. The party started around ten. With a set of binoculars and from the comfort of a conveniently-placed barn, we kept close tabs on the party attendance.

This was a true southern belle party. The girls were wearing summer dresses with pearls and the guys who attended were in their frat boy uniform — khaki pants and navy blue blazers with gold buttons. After graduation these dillholes would be doing air-golf swings outside an unfortunate coworker's cubicle. If this middle-aged frat boy behavior ever happens to one of us, the others have carte blanche to drag his ass out in the yard and put him down with a framing hammer — likewise for listening to Jimmy Buffet or using work clichés like 'thinking outside the box'.

There were appy plates, punch, and monogrammed napkins. Along with the frilly invites would surely come the matching frilly thank-you notes the next day. There would be a designated photo taker who would take the stock cheek-to-cheek photos cheerleaders and sorority girls are taught in their childhoods. The coffee table was covered in a lacey table cloth and being used as a gift table.

At around midnight we decided the party was full and went back to our apartment to prepare the package. Once there, we cocked and loaded the cannon with the sacred caca. With a dangerous cloud of irony looming, this was more nerve-racking than the dry run. Although it would have been disgusting, we did have back up ammo just in case. Ray carefully slid the bomb into the box and connected the trigger line to the lid.

I was the lookout while Brian and Ray gingerly carried the box towards the apartment. The party was on the second floor, and I could see the nervous sweat on Brian's forehead through the binoculars. They set the present at the door and met me at the barn. A rookie would have rung the doorbell in this situation, which would have increased the odds of getting caught and not seeing the punch line.

"What the hell is that noise?" I asked.

"That's my leg jumping up and down," Brian answered nervously. "Damn, I hope this works."

"Someone will come out for a smoke sooner or later," Ray said.

"We should have done a dress rehearsal with the real shit," I worried.

"I think it's a bit late for that, Nate," Ray said.

"There isn't anyone we can really pray to for this type of thing, is there?" I asked to no one in particular.

We waited and waited. I became so excited I started to lose feeling in my legs. Ray was using the binoculars to keep us informed of everyone's movements. We could also hear every word they were saying in the quiet Alabama night. There was nothing too exciting, no drunkenness. This was a classy affair and everyone was behaving like responsible adults, except the three sketch-balls in the barn. Finally, one of the guys came out for a smoke.

"Mandy, there's a really big present out here for ya," the dude said as he lit his cigarette — the cigarette that would eventually save his life. He got a friend to help him carry the box in and set it on the gift table and walked back outside to finish his smoke.

Big M pulled off the card and read it to herself.

"Oh ... they shouldn't have." She then reread the card to her friends who had gathered around the enormous box.

"I know y'all think they are dickheads, but deep

down, they are really good guys," Mandy told the sweet, angelic sorority girls, who obviously found us a much lower class than themselves.

"What is it? It's huge," she said as she reached for the lid.

As she lifted the lid, the universe heard only one noise:

Click.

If I had a choice between reliving the next three seconds of this story or meeting Jesus Christ, I would punch that hippy carpenter right in his mouth. I swear the soundtrack to *Braveheart* was playing in the background.

A millisecond after the universe heard "click", hell rained down on this socialite soirée. The time it took to go from "click" to everyone in a twenty-foot radius covered head to toe in shit was less than a tenth of a second. It was instantaneous.

The shit came out with such force it blew the lid out of Big M's hands and into the kitchen. The cow diarrhea exploded from the box in a large, flat, mushroom cloud. The shit flew in all directions. Everyone, every wall, every gift, every piece of furniture, and every morsel of food was blanketed in a sheet of brown. All of them stood frozen in place looking down at their shit-covered arms. No one knew what had happened. And then the head of their sorority, miss squeaky-clean high society, put it all together.

"It's shit!!!!!!!!!" she yelled at the top of her lungs as she ran towards the bathroom.

People began gagging as they tried unsuccessfully to remove the shit from their faces and mouths, which were possibly open if they were eating or talking when lightning struck. It was as if someone had dropped napalm on their small village. People were running, but had no idea where or how to get to safety. One of the guys was trying to wash the shit out of his mouth with a Miller Lite on the porch.

The three of us could not contain ourselves. We were howling out loud and slapping each other on the back, shocked at how well it had worked. We couldn't move; we did not want to leave this state of bliss. Everything in life at this moment made sense. We were gods. Ever since this moment, life has been miserably incomplete. Maybe she heard us, or maybe she remembered the signed card — either way, Big M was on to us.

"I'mgoingtokillyoumuthafuckers!" she screamed out the door with her voice cracking.

"We've got to get out of here," I whispered trying to pull it together.

"We can't leave yet," Brian said hysterically.

"I can't breathe," was Ray's contribution.

We stayed in the barn until two of the guys at the party came looking for us. I'm not sure exactly what they'd planned if they had found us. This was one of those cliché macho moves frat boys do to impress the girls, yet they have no real intentions of doing anything to help the situation. It wasn't like we left the country; we were "hiding" at our apartment watching T.V. and eating pork rinds less than 75 feet away with the door open. Douche bags.

Like my parents, I hope I am able to ignore the peer pressure of today and let my boys run wild like undomesticated miniature donkeys. Maybe they'll have a scar or two, do something dangerous or stupid — or both. Maybe they won't get a 2400 on their S.A.T. or go to an Ivy League school. And maybe they will not take family portraits on the beach in their khaki pants and white button-downs with the obligatory golden retriever (the prerequisite canine of the white upper-class). And maybe they will not be invited to join a boring, elite country club that smells of decaying skin and mummified flatulence that is run by a man named Biff or perhaps Preston. And maybe I won't fork out the extra dough so they can be taught Mandarin in kindergarten.

Perhaps, they'll learn from their stupidity, be able to wipe their own ass when they head off to college, be able to handle rejection, failure, and critique without a lunch box full of meds. Yeah, they might not make it to Harvard, but maybe they'll have the self-confidence and balls to make up for it. And when it comes to learning a second language in kindergarten, if we're talking about competing in a global economy, I like their chances. A double backflip gainer off a rope swing trumps a bilingual *PowerPoint* presentation any day of the week; I don't give a damn what they teach you in business school.

Back in our apartment, every time we got it together, someone would start snickering and we would start laughing all over again. This went on for hours until we were all hoarse and had cramped stomachs. Things finally started to calm down around 4:00 a.m., and we were all falling asleep on the couches.

"I love you guys," I said in my raspy voice as I drifted off.

"You're a fag, Nate. But yeah, you're right, that was awesome," Ray said.

"Ditto," Brian said, as the sun was starting to come up.

THE END

Afterword:
Relatively Well-Adjusted
Adults

Nathan Weathington has a Bachelor of Civil Engineering and a Masters of Business Administration. He has worked as a developer, teacher, bartender, GM of an Internet company, and a publisher of a variety of newspapers. If you are reading this, he is now a professional shit-joke writer. He met his wife while working in The Bahamas and they live with their two boys in New Zealand.

Brian Weathington has a degree in wildlife management that he does not use. He is now a shit-hot medical equipment sales rep. His two kids are destined to shoot him in the ass with a slingshot at some point. He moonlights as a shit-joke consultant and is still the only person to unquestioningly deliver quality, original material to philosophical questions such as, "Do you know three funny ways to kill a dog?" Brian now calls Birmingham, Alabama home.

Ray Womack has a Bachelor of Civil Engineering and is now a professional engineer and the only project manager who can hotwire the bulldozer if the foreman doesn't show. He claims he can still deliver the Double-Corn-Dog-Ray-Gainer off a rope swing and has yet to be beat in arm wrestling. He and his wife live in Montgomery, Alabama, with their son and daughter.

Marla Harvin née Weathington graduated with a business degree and is now a Montessori teacher. She lives in Charleston, South Carolina, with her husband and their two sons. Although he doesn't know it, she could beat her husband's ass if push came to shove.

Ashley Sanders is now a Georgia State Patrol Officer and is synonymous with the word "Ironic" as well as "putting your foot in your mouth." He moved in next door to Marilyn and Larry Weathington with his wife and two daughters.

Marilyn and Larry Weathington still live in Bremen, Georgia, and travel extensively to see their six grandkids. Larry at 65 can still beat everyone's ass but Marilyn is still in charge as always.

Acknowledgments

Thanks to everyone who has ever laughed at one of my jokes. Although my wife no longer laughs at my jokes, she did encourage me to quit my nice paying job for the untold riches of being a stay-at-home dad and publishing my first book, neither of which I am qualified to do. Morgan, you know how much I love you, I don't have to write it here. Thanks to Jody and Carol for making me sound smarter than I am. And to Evan Pine for summing up my crazy childhood in one stunning cover. Thanks to all the artists, fisherman, and true friends who have helped along the way with their encouragement, connections, and knowledge. If you are reading this, you have helped make one of my dreams come true, and I am truly thankful for that.

About the Author

Nathan Weathington has worked as a civil engineer, bartender, math teacher, GM of a large website, publisher of several newspapers in British Columbia, as well as a sadistic astrologer known as Mr.Asstrology. As an up-and-coming media mogul, he responsibly ditched his career to pursue the untold riches of being a stay at home dad and publishing his first book.

Nathan grew up in Bremen, Georgia, a small rural town that serves as the backdrop for his first book *Where the Hell Were Your Parents?*. While living in The Bahamas, he met his Canadian wife and they moved to New Zealand with their two boys. They now make their home in Victoria, BC.